Developmental Exercises

A WRITER'S REFERENCE

Fifth Edition

Wanda Van Goor and Diana Hacker

Prince George's Community College

Bedford/St. Martin's   Boston ◆ New York

7   6   5   4
f   e

For information, write: Bedford/St. Martin's, 75 Arlington Street,
Boston, MA 02116

ISBN 0–312–40241–4

Preface for Instructors

The exercises in this book are specifically designed for developmental students. Most of them have been adapted from our developmental workbook, *Bedford Basics,* to work with *A Writer's Reference.* A few are new, and all have been classroom-tested.

The exercises in each set are thematically linked, usually focusing on the achievements of a famous person or group — such as Harriet Beecher Stowe, Frederick Douglass, Aesop, Sigmund Freud, Steven Spielberg, or the Beatles — so that students are reading real prose on interesting topics rather than unrelated drill sentences.

Here are the principal features of *Developmental Exercises to Accompany A Writer's Reference.*

Respectful of the student's college status

Although the exercises vary in level of difficulty, all of them respect the age and experience of college students; none insults their intelligence. Most exercises ask students to edit paragraphs and essays, not to fill in blanks or recopy whole sentences when only a word or two may need changing. Where possible, exercises encourage students to think about the impact of errors on readers and to choose revision strategies that are effective, not just "correct."

Written in connected discourse

Because nearly every exercise is a paragraph, an essay, or a set of numbered sentences that are connected in meaning, students learn to identify and revise problem sentences in realistic contexts. These connected discourse exercises mimic the process of revision as it occurs in real life. In addition, they provide a rhetorical context to guide students as they choose one revision strategy over another. When revising comma splices and fused sentences, for example, students will see that relying too heavily on the period and the semicolon results in dull, monotonous prose. They will begin to see the need for occasional subordination, and the rhetorical context will suggest just where subordination would be most effective.

"Guided practice" exercises

Most sections open with a guided practice exercise that gives students special help. Section codes (G1, G1-c) in the margin identify problem sentences and tell students where in *A Writer's Reference* to look for explanations and revision strategies. Answers to these exercises appear in the back of the book.

Varied formats

Seldom will students be asked to do exactly the same thing in two adjacent exercises. Varied ways of working on a topic keep the task interesting. Sometimes students need only to circle the letter of the correct or clearer sentence in a pair of sentences; sometimes they choose between two words or phrases; frequently they edit, crossing out incorrect or confusing forms and adding handwritten revisions; occasionally, they edit the same sentence in two different ways.

Many exercises provide hints for students, telling them, for example, that two of the ten sentences in a set are correct or that half of the sentences use a strategy, such as parallelism, correctly and the other half need revision.

Emphasis on reading

As they learn to edit the paragraphs and essays in the exercises, students do a considerable amount of reading, and many exercises ask them to respond as readers. In an exercise on mixed constructions, for example, students are asked to discriminate between the easy-to-read and the hard-to-read sentences. Where possible, students are encouraged to think about meaning. "Which sentences are ambiguous?" asks an exercise on needed words. "What is the difference in meaning between the sentences 'Most slaves did not find escape routes easy' and 'Most slaves did not find escape routes easily'?" asks an exercise on adjectives and adverbs.

Cross-curricular content

Most exercises profile a person or group that students are likely to encounter in college courses across the curriculum: Mary Wollstonecraft, Albert Einstein, Martin Luther King Jr., Louis Braille, Mother Jones, and so on. Because many of these persons overcame great obstacles to achieve their goals, their stories are often inspirational as well as informative.

Adaptable to a variety of teaching styles

You can use the exercises in a variety of ways. We have used them successfully for homework or quizzes, for nongraded individual study, for class discussions, and for collaborative learning in small groups.

Acknowledgments

We are grateful to several people at Bedford/St. Martin's who were actively involved in the book's development and production. Publisher Joan Feinberg helped us plan the book. Developmental editor Nelina Backman responded to the manuscript, and production editor Anne Noonan guided it expertly through production, with unflappable good humor.

Thanks also go to Claire Seng-Niemoeller for designing the book's pages and to copyeditor Rosemary Winfield for bringing consistency and grace to the final manuscript.

Finally, for their support and encouragement, we would like to thank our families, our colleagues at Prince George's Community College, and the many students over the years who have taught us that errors, a natural by-product of the writing process, are simply problems waiting to be solved.

Wanda Van Goor and Diana Hacker

Prince George's Community College

Introduction for Students

To learn any skill — whether basketball, tennis, chess, CPR, computer programming, or the electric guitar — takes practice. English composition is no exception: In a composition class, you will learn to write by writing, and you will learn to revise by revising.

Developmental Exercises to Accompany A Writer's Reference will sharpen your revision skills by giving you a great deal of controlled, yet realistic, practice. Let's say, for example, that you want to learn to identify and revise sentence fragments. Your first step is to read section G5 in *A Writer's Reference,* Fifth Edition, and to study the flow chart on page 195. Then, keeping *A Writer's Reference* open to section G5, work on Exercise G5-1 in *Developmental Exercises to Accompany A Writer's Reference.* Exercise G5-1, which we call a "guided practice," gives codes in the margin (such as G5-a or G5-c) next to all fragments. In addition to telling you where to look for fragments, the codes refer to specific rules in the text, so if you have trouble identifying or fixing a particular fragment, you can consult *A Writer's Reference* for help. When you have finished the exercise, you should check your answers. Answers to the first exercise in each set appear in the back of this book, beginning on page 165.

Once you have done the guided practice exercise, attempt the other exercises in the set; continue to refer to *A Writer's Reference* when you run into trouble. You'll find that the rest of the exercises in a set vary in style and level of difficulty. In the set on fragments, for example, one exercise asks you to identify the correct sentence in a pair of word groups; another, presented in paragraph form, asks you to identify fragments and to think about possible revision strategies; and the final three exercises give you practice in both identifying and revising fragments. Throughout the entire set, the subject you'll be reading about is the Beatles. Other exercise sets resemble the one on fragments. In those sets you will encounter a number of famous persons you are likely to read about in other college classes: men and women such as Karl Marx, Harriet Beecher Stowe, Frederick Douglass, Albert Einstein, Aesop, and Amelia Earhart.

Wanda Van Goor and Diana Hacker

Prince George's Community College

Contents

Grammatical Sentences

ESL Trouble Spots

Punctuation

Mechanics

Grammar Basics

Answers to Guided Practice and Preview Exercises

EXERCISE S1-1   Parallelism: Guided practice

Edit the following paragraphs to correct faulty parallelism. Rule numbers in the margin refer to appropriate rules in section S1 of *A Writer's Reference,* Fifth Edition. The first revision has been done for you, and a suggested revision of this exercise appears in the back of the book.

In his own time, one famous sixteenth-century man was known only by his given name, "Leonardo." Today he is still known by that single name. But then and now, that name suggests many different roles for its owner: theatrical producer, biologist, botanist, inventor, engineer, strategist, researcher, and artist.

Sixteenth-century Venetian soldiers knew Leonardo as a military strategist. When the Turkish fleet was invading their country, Leonardo suggested conducting surprise underwater attacks and ~~to flood~~ *flooding* the land that the Turkish army had to cross. Engineers   *S1-b*

knew him as the man who laid out new canals for the city of Milan. Scientists admired him for not only his precise anatomical drawings but also for his discovery that hardening of the arteries could cause death. To Milan's royal court, Leonardo was the artist   *S1-b*

who was painting impressive portraits, sculpting a bronze horse memorial to the house of Sforza, and at the same time worked on a mural of the Last Supper.   *S1-a*

Leonardo saw a three-dimensional *s*-curve in all of nature — the flow of water, the movements of animals, and how birds flew. We recognize the same *s*-curve today in the   *S1-a*

spiraling form of DNA. Leonardo invented the wave theory: He saw that grain bending as the wind blew over it and water rippling from a stone cast into it were the same scientific event. It was as easy for him to see this wave in sound and light as observing   *S1-b*

it in fields and streams. The math of his day could not explain all his theories, but twentieth-century scientists showed the world that Leonardo knew what he was talking about.

Leonardo saw very clearly that the powers of nature could be destructive and human beings could be savage. At the same time, he saw a unity holding life's varied parts   *S1-c*

together, a unity he could express in his art.

"Leonardo" — it's quite a name!

EXERCISE S1-2   Parallelism   Before working this exercise, read section S1 in *A Writer's Reference,* Fifth Edition.

All of the following sentences make an attempt to use parallel structure. Half of them succeed. The other five need revision. Put "OK" by the correct ones, and edit the other five to correct faulty parallelism. Example:

> **Leonardo spent the first years of his life playing in the fields, drawing animals and plants,**
> *building*
> **and ~~he built~~ miniature bridges and towers along the river.**
>   ^

1. When Leonardo moved to Florence to live with his father, he exchanged a slow-moving rural life for a fast-paced urban one.

2. Because his birth parents had not been married, many job opportunities were not available to Leonardo. He could not become a merchant, a banker, or a skilled craftsman.

3. It was no easier for Leonardo to attend the local university than learning a craft.

4. The obvious choices were to become a soldier or he could join the priesthood.

5. Leonardo did not want his future to be in either the church or the army.

6. Deciding that Leonardo could draw better than he could march or pray, his father placed him with a major artist, Andrea del Verrocchio.

7. Verrocchio's shop did work for all kinds of customers, including trade unions, churches, and they would do work for individuals also.

8. Living in Verrocchio's home and working in his shop, Leonardo heard talk of new theories about geography and science while he learned painting, sculpting, modeling, and how to cast bronze, silver, and gold figures.

9. Perhaps even more important was the variety of instruments Leonardo learned to make, among them musical, navigational, and ones for surgeons to use.

10. Working with Verrocchio was like going to three schools — an art school, a technology institute, and a liberal arts college.

EXERCISE S1-3   Parallelism   Before working this exercise, read section S1 in *A Writer's Reference,* Fifth Edition.

Circle the letter of the word or word group that best completes the parallel structure in each sentence. Example:

> **Leonardo was handsome, generous, clever, and _____.**
>
> **(a.) ambidextrous**
>
> **b. able to use either hand for most activities**
>
> **c. he could use either hand for most activities**

1. Leonardo's life had three distinct periods: his childhood in Vinci, his apprenticeship in Florence, and _____.

   a. when he was an adult

   b. his being an adult and earning his own way

   c. his adulthood in various Italian cities

2. In childhood, Leonardo had not only a loving family and relatives but also _____.

   a. safe and unspoiled acres to explore

   b. he had the whole gentle slope of a mountain to explore

   c. including fields and vineyards to explore

3. However, two natural events haunted his memory for years: A hurricane destroyed much of the valley below his village, and _____.

   a. a flood washed away much of the city of Florence

   b. a flood that washed away much of the city of Florence

   c. the boiling, muddy, surging waters of a flood

4. Wind and water became major topics for Leonardo's study. He decided that wind and water were not only useful but also _____.

   a. did harmful things

   b. they caused harm

   c. harmful

5. Viewers can find in many of Leonardo's works small round pebbles washed by a stream, riverbanks covered with moss and flowers, and _____.

   a. little freshwater crabs partly hidden beneath rocks

   b. viewers can find small freshwater crabs under rocks

   c. little freshwater crabs sometimes hide beneath rocks

EXERCISE S1-4   Parallelism: Guided review

Edit the following paragraphs to correct faulty parallelism. Rule numbers in the margin refer to appropriate rules in section S1 of *A Writer's Reference,* Fifth Edition. The first revision has been done for you.

Leonardo's vision of life as one borderless unity affected both his personal life and ~~it affected~~ his artistic work.   *S1-b*

Leonardo did not simply look at the world; he studied it carefully. Watching the wind ripple the water in a pond, he was observant, intent, and in a serious mood. Leonardo   *S1-a*
saw no boundaries in nature; to him, people and animals were parts of one creation. He ate no meat because he did not want to bring death to a fellow creature; he bought caged songbirds so that he could set them free. Having no family of his own, he adopted a boy from another family to be both his son and he would be his heir. Even right- and   *S1-b*
left-handedness were the same to him. He filled his notebooks with mirror writing, but he wrote letters, reports, and proposals in the usual way. When his right hand became crippled, he used his left.

Leonardo's view of all of life as one creation led him to artistic innovations. Before Leonardo, artists had always used outlines to separate a painting's subject from its background. Because Leonardo saw everything in nature as interrelated, he decided that using shadow and gradation of light and color was better than to use an outline. He   *S1-b*
wanted one thing to flow into another the way smoke flows into air. Looking at Mona Lisa's hand, for instance, viewers can find no line where one finger ends and the next one begins; the separation is done totally with shadows. This unified vision of the world affected the content of his paintings as well as the technique. Background and subject often echo each other in a picture: The drapery and folds of the subject's clothing may reflect background scenes of curving vines or rocky hills or water that flows.   *S1-a*

Leonardo recognized the great diversity surrounding him, but he believed that an even greater unity supported the diversity and his own work was an expression of that   *S1-c*
unity.

EXERCISE S2-1   Needed words: Guided practice

Add any words needed for grammatical or logical completeness in the following paragraphs. Rule numbers in the margin refer to appropriate rules in section S2 of *A Writer's Reference*, Fifth Edition. The first revision has been done for you, and a suggested revision of this exercise appears in the back of the book.

Mary Wollstonecraft, an eighteenth-century writer, may have been England's first feminist. Her entire life reflected her belief in equal rights for women in all areas of their lives: personal, intellectual, and professional.

From childhood, she never had *accepted* and never would accept the idea that men were superior to women. As a young girl, she knew that her drinking and gambling father deserved less respect than her long-suffering mother. As an adult, she demanded that society give her the same freedom it gave to men.   S2-a

Wollstonecraft also demanded men pay attention to her ideas. She did not argue about an idea. Instead, she gave an example of what she objected to and invited her readers to think about it from various points of view. Working this way, she made few enemies among intellectuals. Indeed, she was attracted and respected by some of the leading intellectuals of her day. Among them she was as well known on one side of the Atlantic as on the other. Tom Paine, the American orator and writer, probably knew her better than Samuel Johnson, the English writer.   S2-b

S2-a

S2-c

Professionally, she was a governess, teacher, and writer. When her father's drinking destroyed the family, she and her sisters started a girls' school. Eventually, financial problems forced the school to close, but not before Mary had acquired enough firsthand experience to write *Thoughts on the Education of Daughters* (1786). As competent or more competent than other writers of the day, she was a more persuasive advocate for women than most of them.   S2-c

Modern feminists may find it ironic that current encyclopedia entries for "Wollstonecraft" refer researchers to "Godwin," her married name — where they will find an entry for her longer than her famous husband, William Godwin.   S2-c

EXERCISE S2-2   Needed words   Before working this exercise, read section S2 in *A Writer's Reference*, Fifth Edition.

Circle the letter of the clearer sentence in each pair. Example:

a. Mary Wollstonecraft felt a woman did not have to marry a man in order to live with him.

ⓑ Mary Wollstonecraft felt that a woman did not have to marry a man in order to live with him.

1a. She never married, or wanted to, her first liaison.

 b. She never married, or wanted to marry, her first liaison.

2a. With Gilbert Imlay, she discovered that travel could teach her much about the business world.

 b. With Gilbert Imlay, she discovered travel could teach her much about the business world.

3a. She had a more intellectual relationship with William Godwin than Gilbert Imlay.

 b. She had a more intellectual relationship with William Godwin than with Gilbert Imlay.

4a. In one way she may have been as conservative as, if not more conservative than, other women of her day.

 b. In one way she may have been as conservative, if not more conservative, than other women of her day.

5a. Marrying Godwin when she became pregnant may have shown that she believed in and acted by society's rules for pregnant women.

 b. Marrying Godwin when she became pregnant may have shown that she believed and acted by society's rules for pregnant women.

EXERCISE S2-3   Needed words   Before working this exercise, read section S2 in *A Writer's Reference,* Fifth Edition.

Missing words make some of the following sentences ambiguous. Add the needed words so that only one meaning is possible. If a sentence is clear as written, mark it "OK." Example:

Mary Wollstonecraft approved of the French Revolution more than Edmund Burke/ *did.*

1. Wollstonecraft blamed women's problems on the structure of society more than the men of her time.

2. Her ideas about women frightened other people less than her husband.

3. One of her daughters, Mary Shelley, who wrote *Frankenstein,* became as famous as Wollstonecraft herself.

4. The readers Mary Shelley attracted were different from those who enjoyed her mother's work.

5. Modern readers know Mary Shelley better than Mary Wollstonecraft.

EXERCISE S2-4   Needed words: Guided review

Add any words needed for grammatical or logical completeness in the following paragraphs. Rule numbers in the margin refer to appropriate rules in section S2 of *A Writer's Reference,* Fifth Edition. The first revision has been done for you.

that

Most people in her era found ∧ Mary Wollstonecraft used very persuasive techniques. *S2-b*

She did not argue and never had by directly attacking those who disagreed with her. *S2-a*

More astute than other women of her day, she used anecdotal "observations." She knew disarming stories and anecdotes would make her point best. Since she did not argue, her listeners never felt they had to defend their own positions and were able to listen to her stories with reasonably open minds. The stories, which often made clever use of allegory and metaphor, came from her own experience and observation. Preferring examples from dressmaking to other occupations, she chose stories that illustrated her points and let the anecdotes speak for themselves. Her technique was as convincing, or more convincing than, outright argument. *S2-b*

S2-c

S2-c

Mary Wollstonecraft's sense of timing was also good. In 1790, she wrote a pamphlet entitled *A Vindication of the Rights of Men.* Part of her reason for writing it was to respond to the excitement caused by the French Revolution (1789–99). People liked her pamphlet very much. While enthusiasm was still high, she produced *A Vindication of the Rights of Woman* in 1792. It, too, was well received.

No doubt part of Mary Wollstonecraft's unusually effective writing came from the fact that she not only believed in but also lived the ideas she wrote about. *S2-a*

EXERCISE S3-1   Misplaced and dangling modifiers: Guided practice

Edit the following paragraphs to eliminate misplaced and dangling modifiers. Rule numbers in the margin refer to appropriate rules in section S3 of *A Writer's Reference,* Fifth Edition. The first revision has been done for you, and a suggested revision of this exercise appears in the back of the book.

people usually think first of

Hearing the name Karl Marx, Russia. ~~is usually the first thought that comes to~~   *S3-e*

~~mind.~~ Marx never lived in Russia at all. Actually, he almost spent all of his adult life in   *S3-a*

England. He was a political exile for the last half of his life.

Marx lived first in Germany. Born of Jewish parents, his university studies were   *S3-e*

completed with a Ph.D. at the University of Jena. His favorite professor tried to get

Marx an appointment to teach at the university. When that professor was fired, Marx

gave up hope of teaching at Jena or any other German university. Marx, because he was   *S3-c*

denied a university position, had to earn his living as a journalist. He worked briefly as

a newspaper editor in Germany.

Next came France, Belgium, and a return to Germany. First Marx and his new

bride moved to Paris, where Marx worked for a radical journal and became friendly

with Friedrich Engels. When the journal ceased publication, Marx moved to Brussels,

Belgium, and then back to Cologne, Germany. He did not hold a regular job, so he tried

desperately to at least earn enough money to feed his family.   *S3-d*

Marx decided after living in Paris and Brussels he would settle in London. He and   *S3-b*

his family lived in abject poverty while Marx earned what little income he could by

writing for an American newspaper, the *New York Tribune.*

EXERCISE S3-2   Misplaced modifiers   Before working this exercise, read section S3 in *A Writer's Reference,* Fifth Edition.

Circle the letter of the more effective sentence in each pair. Example:

   a. Marx almost spent all his time writing, using every waking moment to get his ideas down on paper.

   (b.) Marx spent almost all his time writing, using every waking moment to get his ideas down on paper.

1a. Between 1852 and 1862, Marx just wrote more than three hundred articles for the *New York Tribune.*

 b. Between 1852 and 1862, Marx wrote more than three hundred articles just for the *New York Tribune.*

2a. During his lifetime, Marx did not receive much attention. But people all over the world paid attention to what he had written after his death.

 b. During his lifetime, Marx did not receive much attention. But after his death, people all over the world paid attention to what he had written.

3a. He wanted only one thing for himself: recognition of the importance of his ideas.

 b. He only wanted one thing for himself: recognition of the importance of his ideas.

4a. Capitalist scholars tend to for the most part say that Marx's work is "illogical" and "uninformed."

 b. For the most part, capitalist scholars tend to say that Marx's work is "illogical" and "uninformed."

5a. However, most capitalists agree that as a student of social organization, he was brilliant.

 b. However, most capitalists agree that he, as a student of social organization, was brilliant.

EXERCISE S3-3 **Misplaced and dangling modifiers** Before working this exercise, read section S3 in *A Writer's Reference,* Fifth Edition.

Circle the letter of the more effective sentence in each pair. Be prepared to explain your choice. Example:

> **a. Deciding that there were two classes of people in the world, they were named the "bourgeoisie" and the "proletariat."**
>
> **b.** **Deciding that there were two classes of people in the world, Marx named them the "bourgeoisie" and the "proletariat."**

1a. Convinced that one major difference divided the people of the world into two groups, ownership of property was declared the basis for this division.

 b. Convinced that one major difference divided the people of the world into two groups, Marx declared that ownership of property was the basis for this division.

2a. According to Marx, to be considered bourgeois, a person only had to own some property.

 b. To be considered bourgeois, Marx said that a person only had to own some property.

3a. Marx defined the proletariat as those who owned no property but labored to always produce wealth for the bourgeoisie.

 b. Marx defined the proletariat as those who owned no property but always labored to produce wealth for the bourgeoisie.

4a. After finishing his study of economic history, Marx concluded that history is progressive and maybe even inevitable.

 b. Marx, after finishing his study of economic history, concluded that history is progressive and maybe even inevitable.

5a. Denying God any role in human affairs, economic history was seen as a natural evolution in the world.

 b. Denying God any role in human affairs, Marx saw economic history as a natural evolution in the world.

EXERCISE S3-4   Misplaced and dangling modifiers: Guided review

Edit the following paragraphs to eliminate misplaced and dangling modifiers. Rule numbers in the margin refer to appropriate rules in section S3 of *A Writer's Reference,* Fifth Edition. The first revision has been done for you.

The Communist Manifesto, Marx's most famous work, was written in collaboration with Friedrich Engels, Marx's best friend, just before the German revolution of 1848. It has three sections with distinct characteristics.

In the first part, Marx tries to ~~accurately~~ define terms and to state his basic assumptions. He traces the class systems of earlier times and concludes that there are only two classes in his day, the bourgeoisie and the proletariat. The bourgeoisie are the property-owning capitalists; the proletariat are the working class. Marx asserts that as the bourgeoisie increase their economic power, they work toward their own eventual downfall.   *S3-d*

Set up in question-and-answer format, Marx made the second section of his *Communist Manifesto* resemble a debate with a bourgeois sympathizer. Of course, Marx only sees one side of the debate as being correct. After "defeating" his opponent on major questions, Marx presents his own ten-point program in clear, easy-to-understand, persuasive language.   *S3-e*

S3-a

Marx, after developing the second part in detail, moves on to the final section of the *Manifesto.* He shows how Communists and other reform groups work toward the same goals. Reminding workers that they "have nothing to lose but their chains," Marx calls on them to zealously and actively work together. Marx utters the slogan that can still be heard today in ringing tones: "Workers of the world, unite!"   *S3-c*

S3-d

S3-b

EXERCISE S4-1   Distracting shifts: Guided practice

Edit the following paragraphs to eliminate distracting shifts. Rule numbers in the margin refer to appropriate rules in section S4 of *A Writer's Reference,* Fifth Edition. The first revision has been done for you, and a suggested revision of this exercise appears in the back of the book.

Do you know how slavery began in America or how ~~did it end~~ *it ended?* When the *May-*   *S4-d*
flower landed in September 1620, slaves were already in America. A Dutch ship had
unloaded and sold twenty Africans in Jamestown, Virginia, the year before.

But slavery in America began long before that. Many early explorers brought slaves
with them to the new land, and some historians claim that one of the men in Christopher Columbus's crew was a slave. From the 1500s to the 1800s, slave ships brought ten
million African slaves across the ocean.

Most of the slaves stayed in Latin America and the West Indies, but the southern
part of the United States receives about six percent of them. Few northerners owned   *S4-b*
slaves, and opposition to slavery was evident by the time of the American Revolution.
Rhode Island prohibited the importation of slaves even before the Revolutionary War.
After the war, six northern states abolished slavery at once. Others passed laws to phase
out slavery, and even Virginia enacted legislation encouraging you to emancipate your   *S4-a*
slaves.

But it took a war, a tricky political situation, and a clever former slave to free all
slaves. History gives Lincoln the credit for liberating the slaves during the Civil War,
and he deserves some credit, but emancipation was not his idea. Originally, no one in
government seriously considered emancipation because they were so focused on win-   *S4-a*
ning the war to save the Union. But then a very important black man talks to Lincoln   *S4-b*
and gives him the idea and the reason. This man said that freeing slaves would be good
for the war effort and would Lincoln agree to do it? Who was this man? He was Frederick   *S4-d*
Douglass, fugitive slave and newspaper editor.

EXERCISE S4-2   Distracting shifts   Before working this exercise, read sections S4-a and S4-b in *A Writer's Reference,* Fifth Edition.

A. Edit the following sentences to eliminate distracting pronoun shifts. If a sentence is correct, mark it "OK." Example:

> **Frederick Douglass was born a slave, but he was lucky because his owner's wife did not know**
>   *her*
> **that it was against the law for ~~you~~ to teach a slave to read and write.**
>   ^

1. A slave who learned to read and write gained self-confidence, so they were harder to oversee than illiterate slaves.

2. When he had learned enough to study on his own, the slave Frederick Douglass did so; he used what he had learned to escape from his owner.

3. The master had told his slaves that all escape routes were blocked and that you would have no chance whatever at success.

4. Douglass used a simple but dangerous method of escape; he sailed from Baltimore to New York as a working sailor.

5. A listener could not learn anything about escape routes from Douglass's stories because Douglass told them nothing that would endanger other fugitives.

B. Edit the following sentences to eliminate distracting shifts in verb tense. If a sentence is correct, mark it "OK." Example:

>   *describes*
> **Douglass's narrative tells about his own life as a child and ~~described~~ his torturous beatings**
>   ^
> **by a professional "slave breaker."**

6. Douglass had few ties to his mother and never meets his father.

7. Even when Douglass worked "out" for his master, his master got his wages.

8. His master sometimes allowed him to keep one percent (six cents out of six dollars); the master thought the money would encourage Douglass to work harder.

9. Douglass escapes by pretending to be someone else; he borrowed the identification papers of a freed black sailor.

10. Frederick Douglass used several different names as he escaped slavery; an abolitionist friend suggests "Douglass" to him and Frederick uses it from that time on.

EXERCISE S4-3   Distracting shifts   Before working this exercise, read section S4-d in *A Writer's Reference,* Fifth Edition.

Edit the following sentences to eliminate shifts between direct and indirect quotation or question. Example:

> *whether he*
> **When Frederick was told to choose a new name, he asked could ~~he~~ keep "Frederick" and take a new last name.**

1. When a friend suggested "Douglass" as a last name, Frederick asked whether it was a satisfactory name and did it fit well with "Frederick"?

2. People frequently asked Douglass how did he feel when he found himself in a free state.

3. Lonely and frightened at the time, he said, "I can trust no man" and that he saw every white man as an enemy, every black man as a cause for distrust.

4. Douglass was befriended by David Ruggles, an abolitionist who asked him what did he plan to do.

5. Douglass married Anna and told her that they would move to New Bedford and don't worry because he would surely get a job there.

EXERCISE S4-4   Distracting shifts: Guided review

Edit the following paragraphs to eliminate any distracting shifts. Rule numbers in the margin refer to appropriate rules in section S4 of *A Writer's Reference,* Fifth Edition. The first revision has been done for you.

Frederick Douglass, who was born a slave and became a much sought after lecturer and writer, was a man of strong will and convictions.

Douglass never hesitated to defend the choices he ~~makes~~ *made* for himself and his family. On trains he sat in cars reserved for "whites only" until security officers dragged him away. He walked out of a church when it was realized that none of his people could participate in the service until the white people were through.

S4-b

S4-c

Wherever he lived, Douglass fought slavery. When he published his autobiography, *Narrative of the Life of Frederick Douglass,* in 1845, he was still a fugitive slave. He and his wife moved to England the same year because he feared that his book would reveal his identity as a fugitive slave. Also, some of his other writings had aroused so much animosity that he fears for his life. From England, he wrote letters and worked to gain support for freeing the slaves. After friends in England raised enough money to buy his freedom for him, he was even more determined to help others gain their freedom. (Slaves used to say that a free black was never there when you needed help, but no one could ever say that about Frederick Douglass.)

S4-b

S4-a

Douglass was outspoken in his support for the causes he believed in. When the Civil War broke out, Douglass comes back to the United States to help recruit African Americans to fight. "This war is for you and your children," he told them. Douglass also supported women's suffrage, and he defended the right of members of different races to marry if they wished. When Douglass married his second wife, a white woman, critics complained. He answered them by saying, "My first wife was the color of my mother" and that the second was the color of his father, so he was not playing favorites.

S4-b

S4-d

EXERCISE S5-1   Mixed constructions: Guided practice

Edit the following paragraphs to eliminate problems with mixed constructions. Rule numbers in the margin refer to appropriate rules in section S5 of *A Writer's Reference,* Fifth Edition. The first revision has been done for you, and a suggested revision of this exercise appears in the back of the book.

Sometimes it's hard to separate fact from fiction, history from folklore. Casey Jones, John Henry, Johnny Appleseed, Uncle Sam, Santa Claus — which of these ~~names~~ were   *S5-b*
real men? Although we've been told stories about them all of our lives, but are those   *S5-a*
stories true?

There really was a railroad engineer people called "Casey" Jones; the reason he got
that nickname was because of his birthplace, Cayce, Kentucky. There really was a "Can-   *S5-c*
nonball" too; it was the Illinois-Central's fast mail train. And there really was a train
wreck: Engine Number 382 rammed into some freight cars. The accident was not Casey's
fault, and Casey died trying to save his passengers. When workers found his body in the
wreckage, his hand was still on the air brake lever. (The use of air brakes had recently   *S5-b*
been installed on trains to increase their braking power.)

John Henry was an African American railroad worker of great strength. In legend
and song, he died after a timed contest against a steam drill. By using a hammer in
each hand made him win the contest. John Henry drilled two holes seven feet deep; the   *S5-a*
steam drill bored only one nine-foot hole. The real John Henry died on the job too, crushed
by rocks that fell from the ceiling of a railroad tunnel.

John Chapman, better known as Johnny Appleseed, was a wealthy and well-liked
nurseryman who kept moving his place of business west as the frontier moved west.
His boyhood friend Sam Wilson supplied meat to the United States troops during the
War of 1812. A worker told a government inspector that the "U.S." stamped on the meat
stood for "Uncle Sam." Although it was a joke, but it caught on, and Congress made the   *S5-a*
"Uncle Sam" identification official in the 1960s.

That leaves Santa Claus. As far as historians know now, Santa was not real. But
legends say that there was once a man who . . .

EXERCISE S5-2   Mixed constructions   Before working this exercise, read section S5 in *A Writer's Reference,* Fifth Edition.

Use the technique suggested in brackets to correct the mixed constructions in the following sentences. Example:

What European first set eyes on America? If you say Amerigo Vespucci, from whom the name "America" is said to derive, so you'll be only half right. [*Delete one word.*]

1. Although Vespucci claimed to have found a new continent, but there is no evidence that he ever got to any land in the Western Hemisphere. [*Delete one word.*]

2. Columbus may have seen parts of the Americas first, but when a German mapmaker believed Vespucci's claim and put Vespucci's name on the map explains why the lands became known as America. [*Delete two words and add a comma.*]

3. If Vespucci wasn't the first European to find land across the Atlantic, so who was? [*Delete one word.*]

4. For most British historians who have worked on the question say John Cabot got there first. [*Delete one word and capitalize another.*]

5. Early mariners, a very dangerous occupation, often sailed under several names. [*Insert* who worked at *where it best fits.*]

6. "John Cabot" was the name for Italian mariner Giovanni Caboto used when he worked for the English. [*Delete one word.*]

7. Some people say that Leif Eriksson saw North America first; their reason is because he established a small community on Newfoundland about A.D. 1000. [*Change one word to* that.]

8. Even though Eriksson's community was established five hundred years before the time of Vespucci, Columbus, and Cabot, but the Norse sagas claim that Bjarni Herjulfsson sighted North America before Eriksson did. [*Delete one word.*]

9. The growth in the number of theories increases as new evidence is found. [*Delete three words and capitalize one.*]

10. So who was the first European on American shores? As these bits of history indicate that no one can really answer that question. [*Either delete one word and capitalize another, or delete one word and add a comma.*]

EXERCISE S5-3 Mixed constructions   Before working this exercise, read section S5 in *A Writer's Reference*, Fifth Edition.

Read through each sentence just once. If it sounds correct to you, put "OK" after it. If it sounds like a mixed construction, put "MC" after it. Then go back and check; only four of the sentences should have "OK" after them. Fix the others. Example:

Do you believe that ~~because of~~ Paul Revere's late-night horseback ride alerted minutemen from Boston to Lexington to Concord that the British were coming? *MC*

1. In college, most American students discover that their knowledge of history is a mixture of fact and fiction. _____

2. For example, most students believe that Paul Revere rode alone, alerting citizens from Boston to Concord that the British were coming. In fact, Revere did not ride alone, and he never made it to Concord. _____

3. Since he was able to borrow a horse permitted Revere to get as far as Lexington. _____

4. By adding two other riders, William Dawes and Samuel Prescott, made it possible to get the warning to Concord. _____

5. The vigilance of a group of British soldiers on patrol overtook all three men, captured Revere, and found out who he was. _____

6. The reason minutemen reported promptly for duty was because they were warned by relays of riders who had been alerted by prearranged signals. _____

7. If Henry Wadsworth Longfellow had not written a poem about the ride forty-five years after Revere's death, so Revere might never have become famous. _____

8. Before that poem appeared, Paul Revere's name was not on any list of important people in America. _____

9. The increase in the number of times his name appeared on such lists after the poem was published was enough to make him famous. _____

10. Is fiction more powerful than fact? Is all our knowledge such a mixture of fact and fiction?

_____

EXERCISE S5-4   Mixed constructions: Guided review

Edit the following paragraphs to eliminate problems with mixed constructions. Rule numbers in the margin refer to appropriate rules in section S5 of *A Writer's Reference,* Fifth Edition. The first revision has been done for you.

What did Paul Revere do when he wasn't working for the Revolution? Quite apart from his famous ride, Paul Revere made other significant contributions to American life and culture.

The basic reason for all these contributions was ~~because~~ *that* Paul Revere was an enterprising entrepreneur. He originally followed his father into silversmithing. Soon after the war started, he began making gunpowder. He designed and printed paper money and made the state seal that Massachusetts still uses. By carving false teeth from rhinoceros tusks was one of his efforts to make money; publishing hymnbooks was another. He engraved copper plates for printing. He ran a hardware store and erected barns for local farmers.   *S5-c*   *S5-a*

Until Revere built the first rolling mill for copper in the United States, so all rolled copper had to be imported. He set up the equipment to cast bronze and made cannon for the army, copper fittings for the USS *Constitution* (Old Ironsides), and bells for churches. Seventy-five of his bells still ring from New England church steeples.   *S5-a*

As a silversmith, a very creative field, Revere displayed great talent and skill. His silver pieces were so beautifully designed and crafted that two hundred years later one of his punch bowls brought an offer of a hundred thousand dollars. One reason that antique lovers today search for silver objects marked "Revere" is because Revere's work is so graceful. Modern artisans still try to duplicate his decorated grooves and flowing lines. And shoppers admire certain smoothly curved bowls are known as Revere bowls whether they are made of silver or of some other metal.   *S5-b*   *S5-c*   *S5-a*

Whether or not he rode all the way to Concord, Paul Revere made an indelible impression on American life and culture.

EXERCISE S6-1   Sentence emphasis: Guided practice

Edit the following paragraph to put major ideas in independent clauses and minor ideas in subordinate clauses or phrases. Rule numbers in the margin refer to appropriate rules in section S6 of *A Writer's Reference,* Fifth Edition. The first revision has been made for you, and a suggested revision of this exercise appears in the back of the book.

No one who knew Albert Einstein as a young child would ever have believed that

he might one day be called the smartest man in the world. None of his teachers could

have predicted success for him. ~~Albert was a~~ *A shy,* slow learner~~.~~, ~~He was shy. He~~ *Albert* always got in   *S6-b*

trouble in class. He consistently failed some subjects. They were the subjects he did not   *S6-b*

like. His family could not have predicted his success either. Albert could not even get to

meals on time. Night after night his parents had to postpone dinner until servants,

after searching the house and grounds, found the boy, at which time he would be full of   *S6-e*

apologies but have no explanation to offer for his lateness except that he was "thinking."

Once his angry father dangled his big gold watch at Albert. He told Albert to figure out   *S6-b*

how late he was. Albert, who was fascinated by the tiny magnetic compass hanging   *S6-d*

from the watch chain, could not tell time. The boy asked so many questions about the

compass that he did not eat much dinner anyway. Albert begged his father to lend him

the compass to sleep with, and his father let him borrow it. Years later Einstein won-   *S6-c*

dered whether that little compass had been the beginning of his interest in science.

EXERCISE S6-2 **Sentence emphasis** Before working this exercise, read section S6 in *A Writer's Reference,* Fifth Edition.

Combine or restructure the following sentences so that the independent clause expresses the idea in brackets and everything else is subordinated. Example:

who ran an electrochemical factory,
Albert Einstein's father, Hermann Einstein, had some interest in science. ~~He owned an electrochemical factory.~~ *[Emphasize his father's interest in science.]*

1. Hermann Einstein moved his electrochemical business to Munich; the move made it possible for his son to have the best schooling available. *[Emphasize the fact that Hermann moved his business.]*

2. Albert Einstein's Uncle Jake explained math to the boy and made algebra problems into games. *[Emphasize Uncle Jake's making games out of the problems.]*

3. Albert's mother was impressed by her son's persistent questions and secretly hoped that Albert would one day be a professor. *[Emphasize the mother's hope.]*

4. One of Albert's friends was a medical student at the University of Munich. This friend supplied Albert with well-written modern books on natural science. *[Emphasize that the friend supplied Einstein with books.]*

5. Hermann Einstein kept his business in Munich for several years, and afterward he decided to go to Italy and work with relatives. *[Emphasize the decision to go to Italy and work with relatives.]*

EXERCISE S6-3   **Sentence emphasis**   Before working this exercise, read section S6 in *A Writer's Reference,* Fifth Edition.

Combine or restructure the following sentences so that the independent clause expresses the idea mentioned in brackets. Example:

When
^Hermann Einstein moved his family to Italy, ~~but~~ he left Albert in Munich to finish school.

[*Emphasize his leaving Albert in Munich to finish school.*]

1. Albert was miserably lonely without his family, and he had always depended on them for his social life. [*Emphasize Albert's loneliness without his family.*]

2. He did not get along with the other students. He did not get along with his teachers either. [*Emphasize both ideas equally.*]

3. He had never gotten along well with other students, and they envied his superior work in math and physics. [*Emphasize his not getting along with other students.*]

4. In mathematics he was smarter than his teachers, so his teachers resented him too. [*Emphasize his teachers' resentment of him.*]

5. He was desperate to be with his family in sunny Italy, so he faked a nervous breakdown. [*Emphasize his faking a nervous breakdown.*]

6. Albert convinced a medical doctor to sign a formal request for a six-month vacation. Then he found out that the school had expelled him. [*Emphasize his discovery that the school had expelled him.*]

7. His months in Italy were a welcome change, and they gave him time to enjoy life again and to plan for his future. [*Emphasize that the months in Italy were welcome.*]

8. Albert spent months thinking about his future while he enjoyed Italy's scenery, art, and music, and then he finally decided that he wanted to be a theoretical physicist. [*Emphasize his decision to become a theoretical physicist.*]

9. He knew his father's business was not doing well, but he asked his father for enough money to take the entrance exams at the Swiss Federal Polytechnic School. [*Emphasize his request to his father.*]

10. His father wanted him to succeed, so he found the money somehow. [*Emphasize his father's finding the money.*]

EXERCISE S6-4   Sentence emphasis: Guided review

Edit the following paragraph to put major ideas in independent clauses and minor ideas in subordinate clauses or phrases. Rule numbers in the margin refer to appropriate rules in section S6 of *A Writer's Reference,* Fifth Edition. The first revision has been done for you.

Teachers are not always right about their pupils. Certainly Albert Einstein's teachers, ~~misjudged~~ *misjudging* his ability in math, ~~and they~~ failed to spot the most brilliant student they had ever had. Giuseppe Verdi's teachers made similar errors in judging their pupil's musical ability. Verdi was Italian. He lived in the nineteenth century. He wanted to be a composer. He applied to the Conservatory of Music in Milan, and he was rejected because he "showed no aptitude for music." Today his works are performed more than those of any other opera composer. Scientists have also been underestimated. Everyone has heard of Charles Darwin, the British scientist. This man, who also had trouble in school, first proposed the theory of evolution. He did so poorly at his school, which was the University of Edinburgh, that his teachers considered him hopeless, as a result of which they dismissed him. The first American physicist to win the Nobel Prize for physics was also misjudged by his teachers. Albert Abraham Michelson was a student at Annapolis. He was in the naval academy there. One of his teachers told him to pay less attention to science and concentrate on naval gunnery. Luckily, Einstein, Verdi, Darwin, and Michelson refused to accept their teachers' evaluations of them.

S6-c

S6-b

S6-c

S6-d

S6-e

S6-b

EXERCISE S7-1   Sentence variety: Guided practice

The following paragraphs are grammatically correct but dull. Revise them to add variety. You may need to combine some sentences. Rule numbers in the margin refer to appropriate revision strategies in sections S6 and S7 of *A Writer's Reference*, Fifth Edition. The first revision has been done for you, and a suggested revision of this exercise appears in the back of the book.

Everyone has heard of Martin Luther King Jr. ~~He studied~~ *After studying* for the ministry at Boston University and ~~earned~~ *earning* a doctorate in theology, ~~and then~~ he went home to the South to work as a minister. He started working in civil rights and became the most influential leader of that cause in America. When he died, the victim of an assassin's bullet, his name was almost synonymous with "civil rights." Historians and biographers have recorded his leadership in the fight to gain basic civil rights for all Americans. Many people who know of his civil rights work, however, are not aware of his skill as a writer. King produced other important writing in addition to his carefully crafted and emotional speeches.

S7-a, S7-b (See also S6-c.)

S7-b

King's "Letter from Birmingham Jail" is among his most famous writings. He wrote it to answer a statement published by eight Alabama clergymen that King's work was "unwise and untimely," and the letter shows King to be a man who had great patience with his critics. King is eager to get these clergymen to accept his point of view, so he reminds them that they are clergy. Their goodwill, he says, should help them see that his views hold value. He does not attack them personally. He analyzes their arguments. Then he presents his own views. Does he use many of the emotional appeals for which he is justly famous? No, in this letter King depends on logic and reasoning as the tools to win his argument.

S7-c

S7-a, S7-b (See also S6-c.)

S7-b (See also S6-c.)

S7-b (See also S6-b.)

EXERCISE S7-2 **Sentence variety** Before working this exercise, read section S7 in *A Writer's Reference,* Fifth Edition.

Edit each of the following sentences in at least two ways, to provide varied openings and varied sentence structures. You may need to change other parts of the sentence as well. Example:

a. ~~Martin Luther King Jr. was in~~ *In* jail awaiting a hearing~~, he~~ *Martin Luther King Jr.* read a newspaper article attacking his work.

b. *When* Martin Luther King Jr. was in jail awaiting a hearing, he read a newspaper article attacking his work.

1a. King didn't have much to write on in the jail, so he started writing on the margins of the newspaper in which the article appeared.

b. King didn't have much to write on in the jail, so he started writing on the margins of the newspaper in which the article appeared.

2a. A black trusty, wanting to help King, was able to get some scraps of paper for him after a while.

b. A black trusty, wanting to help King, was able to get some scraps of paper for him after a while.

3a. His attorneys were later allowed to give him a pad of paper. King, fired up by the newspaper article, quickly filled the pad.

b. His attorneys were later allowed to give him a pad of paper. King, fired up by the newspaper article, quickly filled the pad.

4a. King chose to write his response to the newspaper article in letter form, so he seemed like the biblical Paul to some people.

b. King chose to write his response to the newspaper article in letter form, so he seemed like the biblical Paul to some people.

5a. How were King and Paul alike? Paul, a preacher of the Christian faith like King, wrote some of his famous letters from a prison cell.

b. How were King and Paul alike? Paul, a preacher of the Christian faith like King, wrote some of his famous letters from a prison cell.

EXERCISE S7-3   Sentence variety: Guided review

The following paragraph is grammatically correct but dull. Revise it to add variety. You may need to combine some sentences. Rule numbers in the margin refer to appropriate revision strategies in sections S6 and S7 of *A Writer's Reference,* Fifth Edition. The first revision has been done for you.

The famous "Letter from Birmingham Jail" by Martin Luther King Jr. has a clearly

thought-out structure. ~~Dr. King begins~~ *Beginning* with the statement that any nonviolent cam-

paign has to go through four distinct stages, ~~He says these stages are~~ fact finding, nego-   *S7-b or S7-a*

tiation, self-purification, and direct action, *-- Dr. King* ~~He~~ says that he and his fellow campaigners

have gone through all these steps in Birmingham. King tries to reach his readers after   *S7-b*

that beginning by asking them how to answer his children's questions about why they

cannot go to the amusement park advertised on TV. Then the letter discusses the differ-   *S7-b or S7-a (See also S6-c.)*

ence between just and unjust laws, and it emphasizes the need for nonviolent direct

action to dramatize the unjust ones. Next King mentions the "white moderates." He   *S7-b or S7-a (See also S6-c.)*

expresses his disappointment with white religious leaders and white churches who have

failed to join the civil rights movement, but he praises the few who have helped. He   *S7-b or S7-a (See also S6-c.)*

describes the mistreatment he and his friends have suffered at the hands of the local

police, and he gives thanks for the courage of the people involved in sit-ins and bus   *S7-b*

strikes. Dr. King writes finally of his faith. He has faith that the movement will survive

and prosper and that racial prejudice will soon pass away.

Unit review: Sentence style (S1–S7)

Edit the following paragraphs, referring to the section numbers in the margin for suggested revision techniques (see sections S1–S7 of *A Writer's Reference,* Fifth Edition). The first revision has been done for you.

One of the men who greatly influenced Martin Luther King Jr. was Mahatma   *S6-c*

Gandhi, ~~and he~~ *who* introduced nonviolent techniques in Africa and India. Gandhi is called   *S6-c*

the father of his country, and he helped India gain its freedom from England. Gandhi's   *S1-a*

nonviolent method was based on three principles: courage, being truthful, and you had   *S5-a*

to have endurance. By using nonviolent techniques is how Gandhi helped Indians in

Africa and India.   *S4-b*

After studying law in London, he attempts to practice law in India but is not very   *S6-b*

successful. He then went to South Africa to do legal work in 1893. He was abused in

South Africa because he was an Indian who also claimed the rights of a British subject.

Although he had planned to stay in Africa one year, he was there for twenty-one years.   *S3-e*

Fighting injustice in South Africa, the principle of *satyagraha* (nonviolent protest) was

developed by Gandhi during those years.   *S3-e*

After working in South Africa, the Indian movement for independence made Gandhi

return to India to lead it. While in India, he led hundreds of his followers on a march to

the sea, where they made salt from seawater to protest a law that required them to buy

all their salt from the government. He also began programs of hand weaving and spin-   *S3-b*

ning among the poor.   *S2-a*

Although Gandhi believed and lived by the nonviolent principle of *satyagraha,* he   *S6-b*

died a violent death. In 1948 he was assassinated by a high-caste Hindu fanatic. This

man feared Gandhi's tolerance for all creeds and religions. Nevertheless, Gandhi's non-

violent methods have survived to this day.

EXERCISE W2-1   Wordy sentences: Guided practice

Edit the following paragraph to make any wordy sentences as concise as possible without changing their meaning. Rule numbers in the margin refer to appropriate strategies in section W2 of *A Writer's Reference,* Fifth Edition. The first two revisions have been made for you, and a suggested revision of this exercise appears in the back of the book.

Adam Smith, the founder of modern economics, proposed a theory in the eighteenth century that has made him controversial ever since. This ~~British~~ economist, ~~who was~~ born in Scotland and educated in England, wrote the first complete study of political economy. *The Wealth of Nations* was published in the same year that Americans declared their independence from England — that was in 1776. Smith's book pointed out and directed attention to the interdependence of freedom and order, economic processes, and free-trade laws. Although Smith's thinking did not really affect economic policies significantly during his lifetime, its influence in the next century was considerable. Among economists, "the invisible hand" and "laissez-faire" are synonymous with Smith's name. History has only made Smith's ideas more controversial. Say "Adam Smith" to conservative businesspeople, and those same people will smile and make a response with words like "He was a good man — really understood how business works!" Say "Adam Smith" to liberal reformers, and they will grimace and mutter something along the lines of "He was an evil man — really sold the average citizen down the river." Both of these reactions are extreme, but such responses indicate that the controversy aroused by Smith's ideas is still alive.

W2-a, W2-e

W2-e

W2-a

W2-b, W2-d

W2-c

EXERCISE W2-2   **Wordy sentences**   Before working this exercise, read section W2 in *A Writer's Reference,* Fifth Edition.

Tighten the following sentences by eliminating redundancies, unnecessary repetition, and empty phrases. The number in parentheses at the end of each sentence is a suggested maximum number of words for your revision. You may have fewer than that number, but try not to exceed it. Example:

> ~~It is a fact that~~ Adam Smith wanted to find a theory ^to^ ~~that would~~ explain how the economic
>
> world functions. (14)

1. It seems that after many years of study and then years of writing, he published a book that was called *The Wealth of Nations.* (16)

2. This lengthy, protracted book had in the neighborhood of a thousand pages, and those pages included a sixty-three-page index. (12)

3. The full and complete title of his book indicates the comprehensive, all-inclusive scope of the book: *An Inquiry into the Nature and Causes of the Wealth of Nations.* (20. Do not shorten the twelve-word title.)

4. Smith believed that there were certain basic, essential economic laws in existence and that these laws would work to the benefit of everyone if people would "let the market alone." (19)

5. He believed that something along the lines of an "invisible hand" guided economics. (10)

EXERCISE W2-3   Wordy sentences   Before working this exercise, read section W2 in *A Writer's Reference,* Fifth Edition.

Tighten the following sentences by simplifying structure and reducing clauses to phrases or phrases to single words. Do not change the meaning of any sentence. The number in parentheses at the end of each sentence is a suggested maximum number of words for your revision. Example:

> **Adam Smith saw the market as ~~something that was~~ "self-regulating" ~~as long as~~ everyone left it alone. (12)**

with *if* inserted above "as long as".

1. Adam Smith said that there are two laws that govern the field of economics. (8)

2. The first basic, important, essential law that governs the field of economics is self-interest. (5, but can you do it in 3?)

3. The one who is employed wants a higher wage; the one who employs the worker wants a higher profit. (12)

4. The second law, which is the law of competition, works only if there is no manipulation of the market by anyone. (12)

5. Because people will buy the gloves that cost the least, a manufacturer of gloves cannot raise prices for gloves too much without bringing about the result that people who buy gloves go to competitors who sell gloves for a lower price. (25)

6. The term that has been given to Smith's "let the market alone" policy by economists is "laissez-faire." (9)

7. Adam Smith urged governments to practice the policy of laissez-faire with the resulting effect that would allow "the invisible hand" to regulate the marketplace. (16)

8. Smith assumed that there was a "law of accumulation" that worked by requiring industrialists to add buildings and machinery, to hire more workers, and to produce more goods. (23)

9. There was another law that he called the "law of population" that would supply the workers that were necessary. (11)

10. In the long run, said Smith, those who did the work would be paid, the industrialists who employed those who did the work would make a fair profit, and the landlords who rented space to the industrialists would have many tenants. (22)

EXERCISE W2-4   Wordy sentences: Guided review

Edit the following paragraph to make any wordy sentences as short as possible without changing their meaning. Rule numbers in the margin refer to appropriate strategies in section W2 of *A Writer's Reference,* Fifth Edition. The first wordy sentence has been revised for you.

Adam Smith was convinced ~~in his mind~~ that if people would "let the market alone,"   *W2-a*

all would be well. The true facts about how the market operated during the next cen-   *W2-a*

tury would have distressed him. The industrialists chose Smith as the patron saint for

industrialists. Working to make sure that the government "let the market alone," they   *W2-b*

opposed even laws that forbade shackling children to the machines that were operated   *W2-d*

by them. By means of agreements that were secret, they agreed to charge identical   *W2-e*

prices. Similarly, workers agreed to demand the same wages from every employer. Nei-

ther employers nor employees followed Adam Smith's injunction to let the market alone.

It seems quite obvious that there can be no doubt that Adam Smith would be disap-   *W2-c*

pointed in the way his economic theories have been used — and misused.

EXERCISE W3-1   Active verbs: Guided practice

Improve the following paragraphs by replacing ineffective *be* verbs and passive verbs with active alternatives. Rule numbers in the margin refer to appropriate rules in section W3 of *A Writer's Reference,* Fifth Edition. The first two revisions have been made for you, and suggested answers to this exercise appear in the back of the book.

Three books have shaped economic
~~Economic~~ thinking in the Western world ~~has been shaped by three books~~ more   W3-a
than any others: Adam Smith's *The Wealth of Nations,* Karl Marx's *Das Kapital,* and

John Maynard Keynes's *General Theory.* All three books revolutionized economic think-
influenced America more
ing, but Keynes's book ~~has been more influential~~ than the other two. ~~in America.~~   W3-b

When President Roosevelt asked him to help the United States deal with its De-   W3-b
pression, Keynes investigated causes and cures of unemployment. His theory was a
challenge to the "laws" that had supported most economic thinking up to that time.

Adam Smith's "law of the markets" was accepted by economists of the time. This   W3-a
law stated that supply produces demand — that is, if merchants offer goods, people will
buy them. Keynes disagreed, arguing that demand, not supply, keeps an economic system healthy and that unemployment leads to a decline in demand.

Classical economists taught that depressions were the result of lack of goods; Keynes   W3-b
said they resulted from lack of buyers. Classicists said, "If you make it, they will buy."
Keynes said, "If they have the money and want the product, they will buy."

Adam Smith's followers believed that the market would correct itself, that if things
went too far in one direction, market forces would push them in the other direction.
They believed that unemployment would diminish if lower wages were accepted by   W3-a
workers. They also believed that if businesses lowered prices, people would start buying
again and the depression would end.

Keynes said, "No!" He argued that when businesses lowered prices, they would
also cut back on production and lay off workers. The laid-off workers would have no
money with which to buy anyone's products, and things would go from bad to worse.

EXERCISE W3-2   Passive verbs   Before working this exercise, read section W3-a in *A Writer's Reference,* Fifth Edition.

Some passive verbs are appropriate. Writers may use them to emphasize the receiver of the action or to minimize the importance of the actor. In the following sentences, passive verbs are italicized. Information in brackets tells you what to emphasize. Put "OK" in the blank if the sentence emphasizes what it is supposed to emphasize; improve the other sentences. Examples:

_____   *John Maynard Keynes revolutionized the* ~~The~~ field of economics, ~~was revolutionized by John Maynard Keynes.~~ [*Emphasize the actor.*]

___OK___   As a result of Keynes's work, two new terms *were introduced* into the economic vocabulary: microeconomics and macroeconomics. [*Minimize the actor.*]

1. _____   The economic world *is viewed* differently by microeconomists and macroeconomists. [*Emphasize the actor.*]

2. _____   In microeconomics, the economy *is viewed* from the point of view of one business firm. [*Minimize the actor.*]

3. _____   In macroeconomics, the economy *is examined* more globally — from the point of view of the whole country. [*Minimize the actor.*]

4. _____   Of course, no study of economics *can be classified* as strictly one or the other. [*Minimize the actor.*]

5. _____   But the microeconomics approach *has* usually *been favored* by classical economists. [*Emphasize the actor.*]

6. _____   The macroeconomics approach *was favored* by Keynes. [*Emphasize the actor.*]

7. _____   According to Keynes, the government *must be involved* in turning the economy around. [*Minimize the actor.*]

8. _____   Keynes argued that people *could be employed* by the government to build roads, schools, and other public works. [*Emphasize the actor.*]

9. _____   All these workers would create a large "aggregate demand," and the economy *would be revived* by that demand. [*Emphasize the actor.*]

10. _____   Such government intervention *was called* "priming the pump." [*Minimize the actor.*]

EXERCISE W3-3 *Be* **verbs** Before working this exercise, read section W3-b in *A Writer's Reference,* Fifth Edition.

Some *be* verbs are appropriate. *Be* verbs are inappropriate only when they result in needlessly wordy or dull sentences. In the following sentences, the *be* verbs have been italicized, along with any of their helping verbs. Put "OK" in the blank if you feel that the verb is acceptable; improve the other sentences. Answers may vary. Examples:

___OK___ **In Keynes's view, the Adam Smith approach to economics *was* inadequate.**

_____ *opposed* **Keynes ~~was in opposition to~~ any view that left out factors influencing the economy.**

1. _____ According to Keynes, most economists *were* blind to important factors in the nation's economy.

2. _____ For him, these economists' observations *were* in contradiction to what was actually taking place.

3. _____ In his analyses, Keynes *was* insistent on including factors often ignored by other analysts.

4. _____ For Keynes, the distribution of income and wealth throughout a nation *was* a necessary component of any economic study.

5. _____ Social and political issues *would* always *be* integral parts of a Keynesian analysis.

6. _____ Keynes believed that prosperity *is* dependent on investment but that investment alone won't always lead to prosperity.

7. _____ Investments, he argued, *will* always *be* dependent on savings.

8. _____ However, savings *are* a luxury that people cannot afford in hard times.

9. _____ Unemployed people cannot save at all, so their influence on the market *is* negligible.

10. _____ And businesspeople *are* resistant to investing unless they can expect a profit.

EXERCISE W3-4   Active verbs: Guided review

Improve the following paragraphs by replacing ineffective *be* verbs and passive verbs with active alternatives. Rule numbers in the margin refer to appropriate rules in section W3 of *A Writer's Reference,* Fifth Edition. The first two revisions have been made for you.

                              Keynesian economics pulled
Today many historians believe that the United States ~~was pulled~~ out of the Great   *W3-a*

Depression. ~~by Keynesian economics.~~ In the 1940s, economists began to realize that

                                                        did not violate
Keynes's theories had some merit. They also decided that these theories ~~were not in~~

~~violation of~~ capitalism's basic principles.   *W3-b*

In later years, Keynes's ideas found less favor among some economists. By the 1980s, "supply-side" economists had begun resurrecting Adam Smith's theories. These economists were of the belief that sharp tax cuts would make the economy grow so fast   *W3-b* that the government could continue spending money without increasing the national debt. Not everyone agreed, of course. George H. W. Bush once called supply-side theories "voodoo economics," but the theories were embraced so completely by President   *W3-a* Reagan that "Reaganomics" became a new word in America's dictionaries.

The battle continues.

Keynes did not have to work; his investments were successful in providing him   *W3-b* with more than enough income for his many interests, from art and poetry to running a business and influencing public policy. Believing in the ideal of public service, Keynes insisted that wealthy people should work for the public good, and he practiced what he preached. For example, a public theater was built and run by him for many years.   *W3-a*

Keynes said that he wanted the "Economic Problem" to "take the back seat where it belongs," and he looked forward to the day when "the heart and head will be occupied . . . by our real probems — the problems of life and human relations, of creation and behavior and religion."

The name *Keynes* is pronounced *canes.* Perhaps the pun is suggestive of a connec-   *W3-b* tion: Just as people use canes to make their way upon their native earth, so might they use Keynes's theories to make their way within the economic world.

EXERCISE W4-1   Appropriate language: Guided practice

A. The writer of the following paragraph used language that is too informal for the audience — an
educated group of nonexperts. Revise the paragraph by replacing slang, regional expressions,
nonstandard English, and sexist language. Rule numbers in the margin refer to appropriate
rules in section W4 of *A Writer's Reference,* Fifth Edition. The first revision has been done for you,
and a suggested revision of this exercise appears in the back of the book.

                     Englishman
In the 1800s, an ~~English dude~~ named Thomas Robert Malthus became involved in   *W4-c*

economics. He was really psyched about predicting how many more people would be in   *W4-c*

the world eventually and how much food would be available for them. What he figured

out was gross. He said people kept having children faster than men could produce enough   *W4-c, W4-e*

to feed them. There was no way to avoid it. Hard times and wars would do most people   *W4-c*

in. According to Malthus, famine, plagues, and even wars were necessary to knock off   *W4-c*

some excess people so the remainder could have enough food.

B. The writer of the following paragraph, unlike the previous writer, used too much puffed-up language for the same audience — educated nonexperts. Revise the paragraph, replacing jargon,
pretentious language, and sexist language. Rule numbers in the margin refer to appropriate
rules in section W4 of *A Writer's Reference,* Fifth Edition. The first revision has been made for
you, and a suggested revision of this exercise appears in the back of the book.

                          population grows faster than food supplies.
Robert Malthus proved that ~~the progression of population is exponential while the~~   *W4-b*

~~amplification of foodstuffs proceeds mathematically.~~ His cerebrations led him to oppose   *W4-b*

any help for economically deprived people. He believed that by relieving the immediate   *W4-b*

problems of the poor, the government actually made it harder for everyone to feed his   *W4-e*

family. Malthus said that if the government subsidized their basic needs, people would

only have more children, thus increasing the population even more. Then the inevitable

famine or drought would have to eliminate even more people to facilitate the survival of   *W4-a*

a few. Everyone from worker to foreman was caught in the same predicament. It is no   *W4-e*

wonder that when the English historian Thomas Carlyle finished reading Malthus's

theories, he pronounced economics "the dismal science."

EXERCISE W4-2   Appropriate language   Before working this exercise, read section W4 in *A Writer's Reference,* Fifth Edition.

Change the italicized words and phrases in the following sentences to more appropriate language for an educated audience of nonexperts. Consult the dictionary if necessary. Do not change the meaning of a sentence. Example:

> *could not*
> **David Ricardo was another nineteenth-century economist who thought people ~~had to stay~~**
> *improve their social position.*
> ~~*put in their social class.*~~

1. Ricardo and Malthus were *tight, close buddies,* but they argued constantly.

2. They did agree on one thing: The future looked *inauspicious* for humanity.

3. Ricardo didn't *figure it all out* just by calculating population growth.

4. He accumulated statistical *corroboration* for the validity of his theory of economics.

5. His theory predicted that workers would always be *lowest on the totem pole,* that industrialists would barely be able to *hang in there,* and that landowners would always be wealthy and powerful.

6. His theory made the landowners the *bad guys.*

7. In those days, landowners were called "landlords"; they rented land to tenant *agriculturists.*

8. Landlords collected rents; but since their land also supplied food for the country, they held *humongous* power.

9. Landlords would *as lief* die as give up their power.

10. When landlords *upped* land-rent fees, workers had to pay more for bread and the industrialists had to pay higher wages without getting any increase in production.

EXERCISE W4-3   Appropriate language   Before working this exercise, read section W4 in *A Writer's Reference,* Fifth Edition.

Circle the letter of the more appropriately worded sentence in each pair. Assume an educated audience of nonexperts, and be prepared to explain your choices. Example:

a. Malthus did not come up with any suggestions for ameliorating the lot of the common man.

(b.) Malthus did not suggest any way to make life better for ordinary people.

1a. Malthus opposed loans to the poor because he did not believe poor families would ever have enough income to deal with negative savings.

 b. Malthus opposed loans to the poor because he saw no way for poor people to increase their income enough to pay off debts.

2a. Every member of society found that his life was impacted by Malthus's "laws" and their parameters.

 b. No one escaped the consequences of Malthus's "laws": Rich and poor both suffered the consequences of overpopulation.

3a. Malthus saw hope only in limiting marriages; he believed that if marriages were restrained, there would be fewer eventual workers and wages would go up.

 b. The one bright idea Malthus had was to put a brake on marriages; fewer weddings meant fewer kids and eventually fewer workers and higher wages.

4a. Ricardo said that the value added to a product by a man's labor was often greater than the wages paid to the laborer.

 b. Ricardo said that the value workers added to a product was not reflected in those workers' wages.

5a. In Ricardo's view, there was no viable system workers could utilize to improve their lot; they would always be stuck between a rock and a hard place.

 b. Ricardo said that workers had almost no hope of improving their lives.

EXERCISE W4-4   Appropriate language: Guided review

Revise the following paragraph using standard English free of slang, jargon, pretentious language, and sexist language. Rule numbers in the margin refer to appropriate rules in section W4 of *A Writer's Reference,* Fifth Edition. The first sentence has been revised for you.

                                     The
~~The relation between the~~ theories of economists Thomas Malthus and David Ricardo *show certain similarities, but* ~one~ *did not cause the other.* ~~is associative rather than causal.~~ Their visions of the future are quite similar, but each   *W4-a*

arrived at his conclusions on his own. Ricardo predicted a dreary future; he said that

future workers would not have enough bread to buy bread. It was not exactly the same   *W4-c*

picture Malthus painted, but it was equally dismal. A modern scholar, Robert Heilbroner,

once said that these two men "changed the world from an optimistic to a pessimistic

one." Before them, most people believed that the world would just naturally get phatter.   *W4-c*

After them, the natural world seemed to be an enemy of the world's people. Although

both Malthus and Ricardo studied the problem, neither of them could render intelli-   *W4-b*

gible the reasons for the recurring fluctuations in the country's economic well-being.

Nor could any other economist who offered his theories on the subject. Malthus and   *W4-e*

Ricardo saw only a gloomy image of future life. Scrupulously honest, they reported that

vision but offered no solutions to the problems they predicted. For many people, eco-

nomics continues to be a dismal attempt to elucidate the reasons for behavior of phe-   *W4-b*

nomena in the market.

EXERCISE W5-1   Exact language: Guided practice

In the following paragraph, improve word choices by replacing general words with specific ones and revising clichés and mixed figures of speech. Be sure that connotations are appropriate, that idioms are used properly, and that words are not misused. Rule numbers in the margin refer to appropriate rules in section W5 of *A Writer's Reference,* Fifth Edition. The first revision has been made for you, and a suggested revision of this exercise appears in the back of the book.

            dominated
Economics is not totally ~~domineered~~ by men. Even in the 1800s, when Thomas   *W5-c*

Malthus and David Ricardo were the experts, one leading writer about economics was a

woman, Jane Marcet. Marcet wrote for the popular press. One of her favorite things to   *W5-b*

write about was political economy. In her book *Conversations in Political Economy,* Marcet

summarized economic doctrines before 1800. Her aim was different than that of either   *W5-d*

Malthus or Ricardo. Rather than propounding a new theory of her own, she was happy

as a lark to popularize theories of other people. Twentieth-century women have done   *W5-e*

more than write about theories that men have proposed. Some of them have taken the

bull by the horns and charged full steam ahead. Sally Herbert Frankel, for example,   *W5-f*

made the first official calculations of the Union of South Africa's national income. She is

only one of the increasing number of ladies who make careers in economics.   *W5-a*

EXERCISE W5-2 **Exact language** Before working this exercise, read section W5 in *A Writer's Reference,* Fifth Edition.

A. In the following sentences, circle the more specific word or phrase in parentheses. Example:

> **Alice Mitchell Rivlin was an important (person, (economist) in the federal government.**

1. Rivlin worked for (an important government office, the U.S. Congressional Budget Office), where she (secured an important position, became director of that office).

2. She received her B.A. from (Bryn Mawr College, a prestigious eastern women's college) and her (Ph.D., highest degree) from Radcliffe College.

3. Rivlin's first job, at (Brookings Institution, a think tank) in Washington, D.C., lasted (for some time, from 1957 to 1966).

4. Most of her (publications, books) have been (put out, published) by Brookings Institution.

5. Rivlin's interest in government finances carried over into the educational world when she became (a teacher, a professor of public policy) at (George Mason University near Washington, D.C., a university in northern Virginia).

B. Edit the following sentences to correct inappropriate connotations. (Consult a thesaurus, the Glossary of Usage [p. 111], or a dictionary if necessary.) Example:

> *perceptive*
> **Alice Rivlin was ~~crafty~~ enough to understand the interrelatedness of individual budget items.**
> ^

6. She planned to execute a thorough analysis of every part of the federal budget.

7. Rivlin did not claim that federal government services were cheap.

8. What she pushed was the idea that legislators should have easy access to information they needed.

9. She allowed herself no alibi for incomplete work.

10. Rivlin's work has proved conclusively that ladies can be extremely competent in financial matters.

EXERCISE W5-3   **Exact language**   Before working this exercise, read section W5 in *A Writer's Reference,* Fifth Edition.

A. Circle the correct word or expression in the parentheses. (Consult W5-c, W5-d, the Glossary of Usage [p. 111], or a dictionary if necessary.) Example:

> **Alice Rivlin had the skill and (patients, (patience)) to analyze the federal budget; she (planned on doing, (planned to do)) a thorough job.**

1. She wanted her work to have one specific (effect, affect) and she was determined to (try and, try to) succeed.

2. She planned (on making, to make) the budget, that (incredible, incredulous) mass of material, more available to Congress before Congress actually needed it.

3. She had no (allusions, illusions) about the difficulty of the task; luckily for Congress, she proved (capable to do, capable of doing) it.

4. When voting on the budget becomes (eminent, imminent, immanent), members of Congress need some (type of a, type of) clear, easy-to-understand document.

5. That document must be easily (assessable, accessible) to any representatives who (plan on voting, plan to vote).

B. Edit the following sentences to correct any misused words or idioms. Mark the one correct sentence "OK." (See W5-c, W5-d, the Glossary of Usage [p. 111], or a dictionary if necessary.) Example:

> *complement*
> **The work of a government budget office should ~~compliment~~ the work of Congress.**
> ^

6. Members of Congress have been known to get very angry at a budget director whose work was not satisfactory.

7. Sometimes the Budget Office must try and please a representative.

8. The director of the Budget Office, however, must maintain that office's independents from members of Congress.

9. Perhaps Alice Rivlin's style was different than that of some other budget officers, for she got the job done without making too many enemies.

10. In fact, Rivlin's performance at the Budget Office may account for her becoming deputy director of the Office of Management and Budget in 1993.

EXERCISE W5-4   Exact language   Before working this exercise, read section W5 in *A Writer's Reference,* Fifth Edition.

Edit the following sentences to delete or replace clichés and to clarify mixed figures of speech. Mark the two correct sentences "OK." Example:

> *be undertaking too much*
> Would an economist ~~bite off more than she could chew~~ if she tried to find out why better
>   ^
>   *fail to materialize?*
> financial rewards for women so often ~~hang fire~~?
>   ^

1. Rivlin has had more than one iron in the fire; besides her budget work, she has written several books and taught public policy at George Mason University.

2. Rivlin did not sweep problems under the rug to take root there and come unraveled; she dealt with them before they became bigger problems.

3. When Rivlin was chosen as a MacArthur Foundation fellow, it was crystal clear that her talents and dedication had been recognized.

4. Rivlin is not the only modern woman to choose economics for her specialty.

5. Looking for such women is no longer like hunting for a needle in a haystack.

6. It goes without saying that women's roles in the labor market have changed radically.

7. It is a crying shame that the economic status of women has not kept pace with these changes. Why?

8. She may be playing with fire, but Cynthia Lloyd wants to get her feet wet dealing with that question.

9. In so doing, she has made the study of women in the labor market an integral and accepted part of economic analysis.

10. Her studies don't claim that money grows on trees but ask why women's efforts to get their share are always put on the back burner.

EXERCISE W5-5   Exact language: Guided review

Edit the paragraph for use of language appropriate for an educated reader. Rule numbers in the margin refer to appropriate rules in section W5 of *A Writer's Reference,* Fifth Edition. The first revision has been made for you; find and correct the other five problems.

               from

Women economists have been no different ~~than~~ men economists in the range of   *W5-d*

their interests. Jane Marcet was interested in writing about economics for the popular

press, not in developing theories of her own. Cynthia Lloyd's primary concern is for

improved economic status for women in the labor market. Alice Rivlin stays busy as a   *W5-e*

bee as senior fellow in the economic studies program at Brookings Institute in Wash-

ington, D.C. Sally Herbert Frankel's interest is finance, particularly South African

national income. Jane Jacobs concentrates on cities because she believes they have a

significance impact on national economies. She claims that only cities can maintain or   *W5-c*

effect a nation's economic life enough to cause real change. Phyllis Deane intends on   *W5-c*

studying developing countries. She keeps her shoulder to the wheel as she digs deep to   *W5-d, W5-f*

find ways to understand the economies of these countries.

Unit review: Choosing words (W1–W5)

Edit the following essay for problems with word choice. Rule numbers in the margin refer to appropriate rules in sections W1–W5 of *A Writer's Reference,* Fifth Edition. The first revision has been made for you.

Economics, ~~which is~~ a branch of social science, deals with the production, distribu-   *W2-e*

tion, and consumption of goods and services. However, you'd better believe it's not an   *W4-d*

exact science, though economists strive to make it so.

Economists have several aggravating habits. One of the worst is the habit of "two-   *W5-c*

handedness." An economist will say, "On the one hand, interest rates may rise and . . ."

In the next breath, he will say, "On the other hand, interest rates may fall and . . ."   *W4-e*

Harry Truman used to get angry at advisers who talked like that. He once said that   *W5-d*

what he really needed was a one-handed economist.

If the current volume of *Who's Who in Economics* fell off its library shelf, the floor

would be dented by this 935-page book. Hundreds of names are in that volume, but the   *W3-a*

same few keep rising to the top and surfacing. Whenever people discuss economics, they   *W2-a*

nearly always refer to Malthus, Ricardo, Veblen, or last but not least Keynes. But the   *W5-e*

same name nearly always heads the list. Just as cream always rises to the top of the   *W5-f*

ladder of success, Adam Smith's name has led all the rest for two centuries.

Pretend you are the host of a current TV show about money. Pretend also that you

write books with titles like *The Money Game* and *Supermoney.* What type of a name   *W5-d*

would you choose for your *nom de plume?* You would want an easily recognized name.   *W4-b*

You might do just what George Jerome W. Goodman did when he started a successful

TV show about managing money: he called himself "Adam Smith."

Name _Andy Ellison_   Section _____   Date _9/15/05_

EXERCISE G1-1   Subject-verb agreement: Guided practice

Circle the correct verb from each pair in parentheses. Rule numbers in the margin refer to appropriate rules in section G1 of *A Writer's Reference,* Fifth Edition. The first selection has been made for you, and an answer to this exercise appears in the back of the book.

Before reaching college, nearly everyone already (**knows,** know) several facts about   *G1-e*

fables. Most students know, for example, that fables are short stories that (conveys,   *G1-i*

convey) a moral. They also know that fables nearly always have animal characters but

that animal characters alone (is, **are**) not a signal that the story is a fable. They know of   *G1-h*

Aesop, to whom most familiar fables in Western culture (is, **are**) attributed. They know   *G1-b*

that there (**is**, are) generally only two or three characters in an Aesop fable, that a crowd   *G1-g*

of observers almost never (has, **have**) a role in his stories.   *G1-f*

Most adults recognize that the subject matter of Aesop's fables is nearly always

the same. Once in a while, but not often, politics (is, **are**) highlighted in a story. Usually,   *G1-j*

however, Aesop's fables point out the value of common sense or make gentle fun of

human failings. Since neither foolish behavior nor human failings (seems, **seem**) to be   *G1-d*

in short supply, Aesop's stories keep on being told. Besides, they attract a wide audi-

ence: Adults and children both (enjoy, **enjoys**) them. Everyone who has gone to school   *G1-c*

(**is**, are) supposed to know some of Aesop's fables. "The Fox and the Grapes," for in-   *G1-e*

stance, (is, **are**) familiar to many children as a story long before they understand its   *G1-k*

meaning.

EXERCISE G1-2   Subject-verb agreement   Before working this exercise, read section G1 in *A Writer's Reference,* Fifth Edition.

Verbs in the following sentences are italicized. Underline the simple subject (or simple subjects) of each verb, and edit the sentence to make the subject and verb agree. Keep all verbs in the present tense, and do not change the three correct sentences. Example:

> *have*
> **Many of the morals or wise sayings from fables ~~has~~ become a part of our language.**

1. Phrases like "a wolf in sheep's clothing" *is used and understood* by many people. — *uses / understand*

2. The expression "a wolf in sheep's clothing" *comes* from one of Aesop's fables. — *come*

3. A flock of sheep and a hungry lion *is* the main characters in the story. — *are*

4. After killing a sheep for their supper, the shepherd and his helpers *forgets* about the skin from the sheep. — *forget*

5. The wolf, finding the ~~discarded~~ skin, *cover* himself with it. — *covers*

6. Joining the flock, he *pretends* to be a mother looking for her lamb. — *pretends*

7. The flock *accept* him as a sheep. — *accepts*

8. Neither the sheep nor the shepherd *notice* the wolf at first. — *notices*

9. Daily luring a lamb from the flock, the wolf *feeds* himself very well for a while. — *feeds*

10. Everyone hearing the story *understand* its warning to beware of people pretending to be what they are not. — *understands*

EXERCISE G1-3   Subject-verb agreement   Before working this exercise, read section G1 in *A Writer's Reference*, Fifth Edition.

All of the following sentences have two subjects and verbs. The subjects are italicized. Edit each sentence to make the subjects and verbs agree. Keep all verbs in the present tense. One subject-verb pair in each sentence is correct. Example:

> *is*
> *"Sour grapes"* ~~are~~ a common expression, but not *everyone* knows the origin of that phrase.
> ^

1. Aesop's *story* "The Fox and the Grapes" tells about a fox ~~who~~ try unsuccessfully to get some grapes.

2. There are a big ~~bunch~~ of grapes hanging over the top of a wall, and the *fox* is hot and thirsty.

3. A favorite *food* of his are grapes, and *he* leaps up to get some — without success.

4. Hoping that no *crowd* of friends are watching, the *fox* takes a running leap for the top of the wall.

5. Unsuccessful, the *fox* in the story tries again and again with the same result; neither his *cleverness nor* his high *leaps* is successful.

6. Embarrassed, the *fox* fears that *news* of his failures are going to give his friends something to tease him about.

7. The fox's *pride and* his *self-confidence* has suffered, so *he* claims not to want the grapes anyway.

8. The *fox,* stalking proudly off with his nose in the air, say the *grapes* are sour.

9. *Everyone* know that the *fox* does not believe his own words.

10. To save their pride, *people* often pretends not to want what *they* cannot get.

EXERCISE G1-4   Subject-verb agreement: Guided review

Circle the correct verb from each pair in parentheses. Rule numbers in the margin refer to appropriate rules in section G1 of *A Writer's Reference,* Fifth Edition. The first selection has been made for you.

From one of Aesop's lesser-known fables (comes, come) the question "Who's going   *G1-g*

to bell the cat?" The fable "Belling the Cat" describes the long battle between mice and

cats.

In the story, a committee of many mice is appointed to find a way to keep the cat

from killing so many mice. Everyone on the committee (tries, try) to solve the problem.   *G1-e*

There (is, are) many committee meetings and much discussion, but in the end neither   *G1-g*

the committee nor its chairperson (is, are) able to make any good suggestions. Finally,   *G1-d*

the time comes for the committee to make its report at a public meeting. Embarrassed,

the committee (reports, report) its failure.   *G1-f*

At first, there is only silence; no one wants to accept the committee's report as the

final word on the problem. Then a little pip-squeak among the mice (suggests, suggest)   *G1-b*

tying a bell on the cat. The young mouse makes quite a speech in favor of his idea.

According to that mouse, statistics (shows, show) that no mice have ever been captured   *G1-j*

by a noisy cat. The mouse points out that his solution would not cost much; a bell and a

string (is, are) all the equipment needed to give the mice warning of the cat's approach.   *G1-c*

The mouse who makes the suggestion gets a round of applause. The committee mem-

bers, who (wishes, wish) that they had thought of the idea, are silent. Then a wise old   *G1-i*

mouse asks, "Who will bell the cat?" The experienced mice and the young pip-squeak

(is, are) silent.   *G1-c*

It is easy to make suggestions that other people (has, have) to carry out.   *G1-a*

EXERCISE G2-1 Other problems with verbs: Guided practice

Correct any problems with verbs in the following paragraphs. Rule numbers in the margin refer to appropriate rules in section G2 in *A Writer's Reference,* Fifth Edition. The first revision has been done for you, and a suggested revision of this exercise appears in the back of this book.

Almost everyone has heard about Aesop's fables, but most people knows very little   *G2-c*

about Aesop himself. Most of what we know about Aesop is a mixture of hearsay and

conjecture. We do know that he was a slave in Greece. One theory is that before he came

to Greece he lived in Ethiopia for most of his life and that "Aesop" is a much-shortened   *G2-f*

form of "the Ethiopian."

Aesop was not a storyteller then, though he would have loved to have spoken well   *G2-f*

enough to tell a good story. He stuttered so badly that he did not even try to talk. In one

story we learn, however, that he could communicate. One day a neighbor brought a gift

of figs to Aesop's master. Greatly pleased, the master plan to enjoy them after his bath   *G2-d*

and directed that they be put in a cool place until he ready. While the master was laying   *G2-e, G2-b*

down in the bath, the overseer and his friends ate the figs. When the master discover   *G2-d*

the loss of the figs, the other slaves placed the blame on Aesop. They knew that if Aesop

was able to speak, he could defend himself, but they did not fear this stammering slave.   *G2-g*

The master ordered that Aesop be flogged. Aesop got the master to delay the pun-

ishment briefly. Aesop drank a glass of warm water, run his fingers down his throat,   *G2-a*

and vomited only water. Pointing at the overseer, he made gestures that the overseer

and his friends should do as he had did. They drank the water, ran their fingers down   *G2-a*

their throats, and vomited figs.

Although Aesop's cleverness saved him from a flogging, it also made an enemy of

the overseer. Aesop discovered a basic truth about life: Being right don't always help   *G2-c*

one to make friends.

EXERCISE G2-2   Verb forms   Before working this exercise, read section G2 in *A Writer's Reference,* Fifth Edition.

One sentence in each of the following pairs is correct; the other contains an error. Circle the letters of the correct sentences, and edit the incorrect ones. Example:

(a.) **Aesop was sent to work in the farthest field because he had made an enemy of the overseer.**

                                       hoped
   b. Maybe the overseer ~~hope~~ **Aesop would run away, or maybe he had forgotten that the field was next to a major road.**

1a. One day a caravan that needed to find its way to Cairo come by the field where Aesop was working.

  b. The caravan driver wanted Aesop to direct him.

2a. By walking with the caravan until it on the correct road, Aesop, who was unable to speak, earned the gratitude of the leader.

  b. Grateful for Aesop's help, the leader offered Aesop a reward.

3a. Aesop silently refused the reward; he had gave his help without expecting anything in return.

  b. The caravan leader wanted to leave at once because he had lost valuable time on his trip to Cairo.

4a. When the caravan leader said good-bye, he ask the gods to bless Aesop.

  b. After the caravan moved out of sight, Aesop took a nap.

5a. While Aesop slept, the gods restored his speech, proving that good deeds are sometimes rewarded.

  b. When Aesop awoke and could speak, he rejoiced that the gods helps those who befriend strangers.

EXERCISE G2-3 **Verb tense and mood** Before working this exercise, read section G2 in *A Writer's Reference,* Fifth Edition.

Some of the italicized verbs in the following sentences are correct; others are in the wrong tense or mood. Mark the correct sentences "OK" and change any incorrect verbs. Example:

> **In ancient Greek culture, an overseer usually tried to sell a troublesome slave; if the slave *was* sold, the overseer's life would be easier.** *OK*

1. When his Greek slave owner ordered that Aesop *be* sold, it was hard to find a buyer for him because he was so ugly.

2. Finally Aesop *requests* that he be allowed to sell himself.

3. Aesop knew that if he *was* not so ugly, many buyers would be glad to get him.

4. If he *was* going to find a buyer, Aesop would need to be clever.

5. One day a caravan that *went* into the slave-trading business stopped at Aesop's master's house.

6. The caravan driver *asked* the slave owner to sell him at least one strong slave.

7. The driver *sees* that Aesop's muscles were strong, but Aesop's hunched back and ugly face discouraged him.

8. Aesop *realized* that his chances of getting away were slim.

9. "If I *was* handsome, I would not be useful as a bogeyman to scare any misbehaving children," he said.

10. If he *were* afraid, the caravan owner did not show it; he laughed at Aesop — and bought him.

EXERCISE G2-4   Other problems with verbs: Guided review

Correct any problems with verbs in the following paragraphs. Rule numbers in the margin refer to appropriate rules in section G2 in *A Writer's Reference,* Fifth Edition. The first revision has been done for you.

Aesop's death illustrated the implied moral of his last fable: When two enemies

                  is

fight each other, it ∧ wise to watch for a larger enemy of both. Aesop's death came some   *G2-e*

years after one of his owners had gave him his freedom. Aesop could have spent his   *G2-a*

freedom laying around, but he decided to travel to distant lands. During his travels he   *G2-b*

become an adviser at the courts of several kings.   *G2-a*

One of those kings, Croessus, sent Aesop to Delphi to distribute some gifts. The

people of Delphi demanded that he give them the gifts at once. Aesop refuse, having   *G2-d*

discovered that the people of Delphi previously lied to Croessus about their activities.   *G2-f*

The angry people decided that if Aesop was dead, they could distribute the gifts as they   *G2-g*

please. They threw him over a cliff to his death, but not before Aesop told one more   *G2-d*

story.

In the story, a frog invites a rat to dinner. To help the rat cross the river to the frog's

house, the frog ties one of the rat's legs to one of his own. Midstream, the frog tries to

drown the rat. The rat puts up such a fight that an eagle flying overhead sees the

commotion and promptly eats both of them.

"You will succeed in killing me," said Aesop to the people of Delphi, "but a larger

enemy will kill you as well." After Aesop's death, terrible plagues devastated the city.

People believed that the plagues were the gods' revenge for what the people had did to   *G2-a*

Aesop. To this day, the expression "blood of Aesop" refer to an innocent person whose   *G2-c*

death have been avenged.   *G2-c*

EXERCISE G3-1 Pronouns: Guided practice

Edit the following paragraphs for problems with pronoun-antecedent agreement, pronoun reference, and pronoun case. Rule numbers in the margin refer to appropriate rules in section G3 of *A Writer's Reference,* Fifth Edition. The first revision has been done for you, and a suggested revision of this exercise appears in the back of this book.

Everyone has heard of Dorothy and Toto and their tornado "flight" from Kansas to

Everyone also knows

Oz. ~~They also know~~ that the Oz adventure was pure fantasy and that it ended happily. *G3-a*
^

But another girl from Kansas took real flights all around the real world. Whenever she

landed safely after setting one of her many records, everyone rejoiced and sent their *G3-a*

congratulations to her. When she disappeared on her last flight, the whole world mourned.

Not every pilot can claim they have that kind of following. *G3-a*

Neighbors knew that Amelia Earhart would not be a typical "lady." As a child,

Amelia was curious, daring, and self-confident, which made her stand out among her *G3-b*

peers. When her and her sister Muriel were young, girls were supposed to play with *G3-c*

dolls. If a girl played baseball or collected worms, they were called "tomboys" and were *G3-a*

often punished. Boys and girls even had different kinds of sleds — the girls' sleds were

lightweight, impossible-to-steer box sleds.

But the Earhart family lived by their own rules. Amelia's father, who she depended *G3-a, G3-d*

on for approval, bought her the boys' sled she longed for. Then came many fast trips

down steep hills; this gave Amelia a foretaste of flying with the wind in her face. *G3-b*

The closest Amelia came to flying was on a home-made roller coaster. Her friends

and her built it, using an old woodshed for the base of the ride. They started eight feet *G3-c*

off the ground and tried to sled down the slope without falling off. No one was successful

on their first attempt, but Amelia kept trying until she had a successful ride. Satisfied *G3-a*

at last, she declared that the ride had felt "just like flying."

EXERCISE G3-2   Pronoun-antecedent agreement and pronoun reference
Before working this exercise, read sections G3-a and G3-b in *A Writer's Reference,* Fifth Edition.

Each of the following word groups contains a problem with pronoun-antecedent agreement or pronoun reference. Edit the word group to eliminate the problem. Example:

> *Pilots*
> **During World War I, Amelia Earhart listened to wounded pilots' tales of adventure.** ~~**A pilot**~~
> **would describe a particularly daring wartime adventure and joke about their ability to beat**
> **the odds.**

1. After World War I, Amelia Earhart took flying lessons. She was a quick learner, but it was expensive.

2. Besides clerking for the telephone company, she drove a dump truck, which almost doubled her income.

3. Members of her family pooled their funds to buy a gift — a little yellow biplane — for her twenty-fourth birthday celebration; it was perfect.

4. At once, Amelia Earhart determined to go higher than any other woman had ever gone; they had never reached 14,000 feet.

5. They had to make a new entry in the record book: Amelia Earhart had flown 14,000 feet high.

6. She often put her little plane through a dangerous maneuver while worried spectators wondered if she could handle it.

7. At first everyone was surprised when they saw her deliberately put her plane into a spin.

8. Each spectator would gasp when they heard her cut the engine off in a spin.

9. But Amelia Earhart repeatedly pulled the plane out of its spin and landed safely, which delighted everyone.

10. Amelia Earhart soon learned that when someone owns a plane, they need a lot of money.

EXERCISE G3-3 **Pronoun case** Before working this exercise, read sections G3-c and G3-d in *A Writer's Reference,* Fifth Edition.

Six of the following sentences have errors in pronoun case. Find and fix the errors. Mark "OK" next to the correct sentences. Example:

> *her,*
> **When the little yellow biplane was sold, it had known only one pilot — ~~she~~, Amelia Earhart.**
> ^

1. Amelia Earhart was the first woman ever to cross the Atlantic in a plane. Only her and the two-man crew were on the plane.

2. The long, dangerous flight frightened all of them — the pilot, the mechanic, and herself.

3. The pilot and her both knew that the plane nearly ran out of gas before it landed.

4. People wondered about who paid for this flight. It was not her.

5. Earhart was, however, the one who received a free ride, fame, and job offers.

6. Earhart, for whom the flight had special importance, was delighted with the whole experience.

7. Afterward, she wrote a book about the flight; the book brought her a publisher, George Putnam.

8. Putnam and her became more than business partners; they became husband and wife.

9. Putnam was a man who everyone respected for his business acumen.

10. He also understood Amelia Earhart's fierce independence and respected her for it.

EXERCISE G3-4   Pronouns: Guided review

Edit the following paragraphs for problems with pronoun-antecedent agreement, pronoun reference, and pronoun case. Rule numbers in the margin refer to appropriate rules in section G3 of *A Writer's Reference,* Fifth Edition. The first revision has been done for you.

                                                        her

Amelia Earhart believed that every woman had a right to follow ~~their~~ own special   *G3-a*

interests, and she urged women to get into the aviation field. Her and a friend even   *G3-c*

formed a national organization for "flying women." They promoted flying for both its

commercial and recreational value; this was a new approach to recruiting women to the   *G3-b*

field. After all, who had made the first solo flight from Honolulu to the United States?

Amelia Earhart. From Los Angeles to Mexico City? And from Mexico City to New Jer-

sey? It was her, Amelia Earhart. No woman ever did more to prove that they could   *G3-c, G3-a*

handle jobs traditionally reserved for men.

    Amelia Earhart's last "first" was never completed. In 1937, she tried to fly around

the world at the equator, which no one had ever done before. She disappeared some-   *G3-b*

where over the Pacific. More than 265,000 miles of air and sea space were searched, but

they found nothing.   *G3-b*

    Amelia Earhart herself is gone, but her influence on aviation and particularly on

women in aviation will endure. She acted on her belief that everyone had the ability to

reach their goals. In 1994, Vicki Van Meter, a twelve-year-old girl, became the youngest   *G3-a*

female pilot to fly across the Atlantic. Fifty-seven years after her disappearance, Van   *G3-b*

Meter took off from Augusta, Maine, from the very spot where Amelia Earhart, who Van   *G3-d*

Meter idolized, had started her flight across the Atlantic. Like Amelia Earhart's, hers

was a difficult flight. Every pilot worries about ice on their plane's wings, and Vicki was   *G3-a*

no exception. Ice forced her to stay close to the sea for a portion of her flight. When Vicki

landed safely in Glasgow, everyone there offered their congratulations — and told her   *G3-a*

that her parents, coming by commercial plane, would arrive a couple of hours later.

EXERCISE G4-1   Adjectives and adverbs: Guided practice

Edit the following paragraphs for correct use of adjectives and adverbs. Rule numbers in the margin refer to appropriate rules in section G4 of *A Writer's Reference,* Fifth Edition. The first revision has been done for you, and an answer to this exercise appears in the back of the book.

Novelists have often used their storytelling talents to influence people's thinking. Charles Dickens did it in nineteenth-century England. From *David Copperfield* to *Oliver Twist,* book after book depicted the plight of the poor and other ~~real~~ *really* unfortunate members of society. Harriet Beecher Stowe did it in nineteenth-century America, but with not hardly as many books. Her *Uncle Tom's Cabin* depicted slavery so well that the book was very influential in causing the Civil War.

G4-a

G4-d

Harriet Beecher Stowe considered slavery sinful and wanted her book to help end slavery quick and peaceful. People first read parts of the novel ten years before the beginning of the war. An abolitionist magazine published it a few chapters at a time, hoping the effect of the story would make readers feel so badly about slavery that they would rally to the abolitionist cause. Many people, reading *Uncle Tom's Cabin* installment by installment, did become convinced that nothing could be worser than living in slavery on a southern plantation.

G4-a

G4-b

G4-c

None of the abolitionists, who devoted their energy to abolishing slavery, expected a more perfect world when the book itself was published in 1852. But they certainly hoped that the book would be influential. It was. Of all the novels published that year, it was the best seller on both sides of the Atlantic. Its popularity was good news for the abolitionists. Harriet Beecher Stowe's wish came true.

G4-c

EXERCISE G4-2 **Adjectives and adverbs** Before working this exercise, read section G4 in *A Writer's Reference,* Fifth Edition.

Both sentences in each of the following pairs are grammatically correct. The sentences mean different things because one uses an adjective, the other an adverb. Read both sentences carefully to understand their meaning. Then circle the letter of the sentence that answers the question and be prepared to explain what the other sentence means. Example:

Which sentence means that southerners thought the book itself was dishonest?

(a.) **Many southerners did not consider *Uncle Tom's Cabin* honest.**

b. **Many southerners did not consider *Uncle Tom's Cabin* honestly.**

1. In which sentence did the people do a poor job of judging?

   a. Those people judged Mrs. Stowe's depiction of slave life inaccurate.

   b. Those people judged Mrs. Stowe's depiction of slave life inaccurately.

2. Which sentence says that the slaves had trouble finding the escape routes?

   a. Most slaves did not find their escape routes easy.

   b. Most slaves did not find their escape routes easily.

3. In which sentence do northerners think Stowe herself was honest?

   a. Most northerners believed Mrs. Stowe honest.

   b. Most northerners believed Mrs. Stowe honestly.

4. In which sentence did the law not consider one person to have just as many rights as another?

   a. Southern judges did not consider all people equal.

   b. Southern judges did not consider all people equally.

5. Which sentence says that the overseers were looking scared?

   a. Rumors of escaping slaves made overseers look anxious in the fields and forests.

   b. Rumors of escaping slaves made overseers look anxiously in the fields and forests.

EXERCISE G4-3   Adjectives and adverbs   Before working this exercise, read section G4 in *A Writer's Reference,* Fifth Edition.

Six of the adjectives and adverbs in the following paragraphs are not used correctly. The first one has been corrected. Find and correct the other five.

Uncle Tom's Cabin was ~~real~~ ^{really} popular, even though it was a very long book. When it was published as a serial in the abolitionist magazine *National Era* in 1851 and 1852, people probably read all of it. But when the novel was published as a book, many people did not have enough time to read it. Since it had been a best-seller, enterprising publishers brought out new, abridged copies for more faster reading. By the end of the Civil War, many people knew the story of *Uncle Tom's Cabin* only from these shorter versions of it — both novels and plays.

Unfortunately, their knowledge was not only incomplete; it was distorted. Publishers left out important sections of this most priceless story. For example, in the book, Uncle Tom works for three different owners, two of whom treat him fairly good. But in the shortened versions of the story, Tom works for only one owner, who treats him very cruel. Even insensitive readers rightly found this cruel owner, Simon Legree, vicious and judged all slave owners by that one. What had been a subplot in the novel — the story of George, Eliza, their baby, and the family's attempted escape to freedom in Canada — became a major portion of the story. Playwrights favored such dramatic subplots and incidents because they were easily dramatized.

Modern readers are often real surprised when they read the entire novel, a book that American critic Edmund Wilson called "a much more remarkable book than one had ever been allowed to suspect."

EXERCISE G4-4   Adjectives and adverbs: Guided review

Edit the following paragraph for correct use of adjectives and adverbs. Rule numbers in the margin refer to appropriate rules in section G4 in *A Writer's Reference,* Fifth Edition. The first revision has been done for you.

Playwrights often find popular novels suitable for the stage. Produced as a play,

most successful

Uncle Tom's Cabin was the ~~successfulest~~ stage play of the 1800s. The play used only the   *G4-c*

real dramatic portions of the novel and therefore somewhat slanted its basic message.   *G4-a*

Even worse than the plays were the "Tom Shows" that toured small towns all over the

North; these shows didn't have scarcely anything but the violent scenes. Audiences felt   *G4-d*

very badly when they watched George and Eliza's desperate escape over the ice with   *G4-b*

their baby. Dramatists played on their viewers' sympathy with the plight of this slave

family. Viewers hoped until the very end that the family's escape would work out per-   *G4-a*

fect. Distortion was bad in both the plays and the Tom Shows, but it was worse in the

Tom Shows, which turned this most unique story of slavery in the South into little more   *G4-c*

than propaganda. Particularly moving scenes from the story continue to be used in

plays and musicals. *The King and I* made use of several. If a modern movie is ever made

from *Uncle Tom's Cabin,* the movie will no doubt reflect the same distortions present in

the old plays and the Tom Shows — and will probably be just as popular.

EXERCISE G5-1   Sentence fragments: Guided practice

Edit the following paragraphs to eliminate sentence fragments. Rule numbers in the margin refer to appropriate rules in section G5 of *A Writer's Reference,* Fifth Edition. The first revision has been done for you, and a suggested revision of this exercise appears in the back of the book.

Four

~~How four~~ young Englishmen added a word to the world's vocabulary in the 1960s. *G5-a*
A word that became synonymous with the 1960s. Especially with the music of that *G5-b, G5-c*
time. That word was, of course, "Beatles." The Beatles became the most famous popular
musical group of the twentieth century. And held the loyalty of many fans into the next *G5-c*
century.

The Beatles were popular in Liverpool, England, and in Hamburg, Germany. Be- *G5-a*
fore they came to America on tour and became world-famous. Liverpool and Hamburg
loved the four young men and their music. The Beatles' favorite club was the Cavern in
Liverpool. Where they hung out together, played day and night, and attracted many *G5-a*
fans. A Liverpool disk jockey first called attention to them, and a Liverpool music critic
and record store owner became their first manager. The disk jockey called them "fantastic." Saying that they had "resurrected original rock 'n' roll." The music critic who be- *G5-b*
came their manager, Brian Epstein, made them shape up as a group. Promoting them,
arranging club dates for them, and badgering record companies for them. He was deter- *G5-b*
mined to win a recording contract for this exciting new group.

In England, the record buying led to the publicity. In America, the publicity led to
the record buying. Everyone wanted copies of the original singles. "Love Me Do," "Please, *G5-c*
Please Me," and "From Me to You." In America, audiences made so much noise that no
one could hear the music. Crowds of screaming teenagers surrounded the Beatles wherever they went. Determined to touch one or more of these famous music makers. Re- *G5-b*
porters observing the conduct of fans at Beatles' concerts found that they had to invent
another word. To describe the wild, almost insane behavior of the fans. They called it *G5-b*
"Beatlemania."

EXERCISE G5-2 **Sentence fragments** Before working this exercise, read section G5 in *A Writer's Reference,* Fifth Edition.

Each of the following word groups includes a subordinating word. One word group in each pair contains a fragment. Mark each complete sentence "OK" and write "frag" after each fragment. Example:

> **a. John Lennon lived with his Aunt Mimi until he was grown. Because his parents had separated and his mother had given John to Mimi.** *frag*

> **b. His father took him from Mimi when John was about five. Because his mother returned him to Mimi, he grew up as Mimi's child.** *OK*

1a. When John Lennon was a teenager, his mother, Julia, began to pay attention to him.

 b. When Julia, John Lennon's mother, bought him a guitar and let him stay with her instead of his Aunt Mimi.

2a. Although he studied art in college, he soon became more interested in music.

 b. Although Julia encouraged his music and put up with the boyish pranks that annoyed Aunt Mimi.

3a. His mother died before he was full grown. While John was still in college, in fact.

 b. Mimi's husband, his uncle, had died while John still lived with them.

4a. John asked Paul McCartney to join his group, and later Paul brought in George Harrison, and all three asked Ringo Starr to join them. Before they cut their first record.

 b. In their early days, the Beatles copied people like Elvis Presley and Little Richard. Before these English boys even visited America, they sang with American accents.

5a. The Beatles gave one reason for quitting their tours in 1966. That the tours were wrecking their playing.

 b. Stopping the tours gave the Beatles an opportunity to do something they had never done. That was to learn to read musical notes and write their own music.

EXERCISE G5-3 **Sentence fragments** Before working this exercise, read section G5 in *A Writer's Reference,* Fifth Edition.

Underline each fragment in the following paragraphs. (Consult the chart on p. 195 of *A Writer's Reference* if necessary.) Do not correct the errors, but be prepared to discuss possible revision strategies for each fragment. The first fragment is underlined for you.

Paul McCartney wrote many of the Beatles' songs. A good student who learned quickly, he began composing songs when he was about fourteen.

Paul said that sometimes a song just came to him, like "Eleanor Rigby." <u>One of his most famous and moving songs.</u> The song is about a lonely woman who can't connect with other people. Paul was sitting at the piano not working on anything special. Just fooling around with melodies and rhythms. Then some notes played themselves in his head and so did some words. Like "Daisy Hawkins picks up the rice in the church where a wedding has been." Later Paul saw the name "Rigby" on a shop in Bristol. And decided he liked that name better than "Hawkins," especially with "Eleanor" instead of "Daisy." He and John Lennon finished the song together.

Paul wrote "Hey, Jude" in an effort to help John's son, Julian, who was upset over his parents' separation. Paul wanted the boy not to be sad. "To take a sad song and make it better." He decided to change "Julian" to "Jude" after he finished the song. Because he wanted the song to have a country and western feel.

All of the Beatles wrote songs, and often they collaborated on one, but Paul McCartney and John Lennon wrote most of the songs the Beatles sang.

EXERCISE G5-4   Sentence fragments   Before working this exercise, read section G5 in *A Writer's Reference,* Fifth Edition.

Correct the fragments in the following paragraphs. The first revision has been done for you. Find and revise ten more fragments.

George Harrison was known in school for two things*/*, ~~His~~ *his* sharp clothes and his love of the guitar. His mother said he sometimes practiced the guitar for hours. Not stopping until his fingers were bleeding. When George met John Lennon, he found another guitar lover. Although they went to the same school, they did not meet there. Because George was two years younger and they had no classes together. Instead, they met on the school bus. After they became friends, they spent most of their time at George's house, playing their guitars.

When George, John, Paul McCartney, and Ringo Starr formed a group, the four experimented with all kinds of things. From melodies and sounds to drugs. George, however, began to want more out of life. To find answers to the big questions he had about war and loneliness and reasons for living. The others agreed to search with him, and George Harrison became their guide.

Later, George and his wife went to India. Where a religious festival they attended impressed them deeply. When George returned to England, he read many books about meditation. And went to hear Indian holy teachers. He shared what he read and heard with the other Beatles. Who were just as interested as George was. When George learned that a holy man called the Maharishi was going to speak on transcendental meditation, he told his friends. They all went to listen to him. To learn whatever they could that would help them.

The Beatles were headed in a new direction. A direction that was obvious in their next album, *Sgt. Pepper's Lonely Hearts Club Band.* The album had innovative lyrics and an amazing musical background. A forty-one-piece orchestra, guitar, sitar, doubled voices, a comb-and-paper instrument, and all kinds of electronic and percussion tricks. The Beatles were no longer copycat rock 'n' rollers.

EXERCISE G5-5 Sentence fragments   Before working this exercise, read section G5 in *A Writer's Reference,* Fifth Edition.

Half of the following word groups are complete sentences. The other half contain fragments. Correct the fragments, and mark the complete sentences "OK." Example:

> *because*
> **As a child and a teenager, Ringo Starr spent a total of three years in the hospital. ~~Because~~ of**
> ^
> **two severe health problems.**

1. Ringo Starr's first hospitalization lasted for a year. After his appendix burst when he was only six years old.

2. Doctors had to perform several operations; Ringo could not attend school at all that year.

3. His babysitter taught him to read and write, so he did not fall too far behind in his schoolwork.

4. When he was thirteen, Ringo had to go back into the hospital. And stay there for two years while doctors treated a lung condition.

5. Now fifteen, he worked at various jobs. But what he really liked best was playing the drums for his many fans.

6. Teaching himself on drums he bought on the installment plan, he played with different musical groups in Liverpool, including the Beatles.

7. When Ringo joined the Beatles, not everyone was sure that he could handle the job. For example, George Martin, who invited them to London to record.

8. Martin insisted on a standby drummer as insurance. Someone ready to step in just in case Ringo was not good enough.

9. Ringo's many devoted fans were not surprised when he handled the job and became a full-fledged Beatle, making new friends at every engagement.

10. Many people considered him the most likable member of the group. Because of his easy smile and his open approach to life.

EXERCISE G5-6   Sentence fragments: Guided review

Find and correct the sentence fragments in the following paragraphs. Rule numbers in the margin refer to appropriate rules in section G5 of *A Writer's Reference,* Fifth Edition. The first revision has been done for you.

Many people influenced the Beatles in their career. For example, Bob Waller, a disk — G5-c

jockey in Liverpool, ~~He~~ first called attention to them in one of his articles. "They resur-

rected original rock 'n' roll," he wrote. When he first heard them in 1961. From Stu — G5-a

Sutcliffe, a talented musician who sometimes played with them, the Beatles copied sev-

eral things. Their hairstyle, their dress, and much of their philosophy. George Martin, — G5-c

who produced their records, advised them how to improve after their early records. And

taught them how to use tapes. — G5-c

The person who influenced them most, however, was Brian Epstein. Owner of some — G5-b

record stores and reviewer of new records. When a customer asked for a record by a

group Epstein had never heard of, he went from club to club. Looking for a group calling — G5-b

itself "The Beatles." By the end of 1961, he had become the group's manager. Convinced — G5-b

that he had found talented and original musicians. His contract said that he was to

promote the Beatles and arrange their tours and club dates. His other duty was really

the most important. To get record contracts for them. — G5-b

Epstein did far more than his contract called for. He made the young men wear

suits every time they performed. Until their gray, collarless outfits became a symbol of — G5-a

the Beatles. He made another demand of them. That they be on time for appearances. — G5-a

He even made them quit chewing gum on the stage. And by the time he had done all

these things, he had also gotten them a recording date. Why were the Beatles so devas-

tated by Epstein's death? When Brian Epstein was found dead of an accidental drug

overdose in 1967. The Beatles lost far more than a good manager. They lost a close — G5-a

friend and mentor.

EXERCISE G6-1   Run-on sentences: Guided practice

Edit the following paragraphs to eliminate run-on sentences. Rule numbers in the margin refer to appropriate rules in section G6 of *A Writer's Reference,* Fifth Edition. The first sentence has been done for you, and a suggested revision of this exercise appears in the back of the book.

Have you ever heard of the Wobblies/ *? not* many people have these days. That's a   G6-c

shame they did at least two things for which they should be remembered. They prob-   G6-d

ably saved the labor movement in America, they definitely gave American folk music   G6-a

some of its most unforgettable songs. No one really knows how they got their nickname   G6-a

almost everyone knows a song or two that they inspired.

The Wobblies were the members of the Industrial Workers of the World (IWW),   G6-d

this union was a small but militant coalition of radical labor groups. The Wobblies could

not get along with the major union groups of the day, in fact, they alienated most of   G6-b

those groups.

The major unions disliked the Wobblies immensely, nevertheless they learned some   G6-d

valuable lessons from them. The first lesson was to avoid getting involved in politics. If

there was one thing the Wobblies hated more than capitalism, it was politics. The Wobblies

avoided politics for one good reason, they believed that political affiliation caused the   G6-b

death of unions. What else did the major unions learn, they learned to deal realistically   G6-c

with workers' problems. Major unions also learned new recruiting techniques from the

Wobblies. In addition, they copied the Wobblies in devoting their energy to nuts-and-

bolts issues affecting the workers.

The major unions never recognized their debt to the Wobblies, the debt was still   G6-a

there for later historians to see. Historians began to compile the story of the American

labor unions, then they finally recognized the contributions of the Wobblies.   G6-d

EXERCISE G6-2   Run-on sentences   Before working this exercise, read section G6 in
A Writer's Reference, Fifth Edition.

One sentence in each of the following pairs is a run-on sentence. Find and correct the error, using an
effective revision strategy. Mark the correct sentence "OK." Example:

> *Although*
> a. Joe Hill may not have been the first martyr of the labor movement, ~~however,~~ he was cer-
>   ^
> tainly its most skillful worker with words and music.

> b. Before his arrest in 1914 for killing a grocer in Salt Lake City, Joe Hill was simply the
>   Swedish immigrant Joseph Hillstrom; no one knew or cared much about him.   *OK*

1a. Ralph Chaplin was the only person who wrote anything about Joe Hill before Hill's execution,
    he jotted down just a few notes based on an interview with a drunken sailor.

 b. Serious historical research has not confirmed or denied those notes because researchers have
    turned up quite different stories.

2a. All the evidence introduced at Hill's trial was circumstantial; furthermore, the dead man's son,
    who had witnessed the murder, refused to identify Hill as the gunman.

 b. Did the state hide evidence it certainly seemed that way.

3a. One Wobbly told the police that he had been with Joe Hill in another location on the night of
    the murder, he also told a detective he could prove Hill's innocence.

 b. That man was promptly arrested and held in jail for the duration of the trial.

4a. At the end of the trial the man was released and ordered to get out of the state.

 b. Hill's own attorneys did not do much to help him their attitude was as negative as that of the
    prosecutors.

5a. Because of their negative attitude, Hill discharged both of the attorneys who were supposed to
    be defending him.

 b. "I have three prosecutors here, I intend to get rid of two of them," he said.

6a. The state never showed a motive for the murder; furthermore, much evidence that Hill's attor-
    neys could have used was never introduced.

 b. How did Hill get that bullet wound in his chest, he told the doctor he had gotten it in a fight
    over a woman.

7a. The doctor who treated Hill was not asked to testify about medical aspects of the case, as a matter of fact, his testimony would probably have prevented Hill's conviction.

b. Protests about Hill's conviction came from all over the world, but they were ignored.

8a. Important political figures tried to help Hill, hoping until the last minute that they could save him.

b. The Swedish consul pleaded for him, President Wilson sent telegrams to the governor of Utah.

9a. Legend has it that Hill's last words before the firing squad were "Don't mourn for me; organize," in fact, he said, "Yes, aim! Let her go! Fire!"

b. If Joe Hill is known at all today, it is probably because of Joe Glazer, his guitar, and the song "Joe Hill."

10a. Glazer was not the composer of "Joe Hill" its composers were Earl Robinson and Alfred Hayes.

b. Glazer, however, made the song known across America, singing it at banquets as well as on picket lines.

EXERCISE G6-3 **Run-on sentences** Before working this exercise, read section G6 in *A Writer's Reference,* Fifth Edition.

Correct each run-on sentence using the method of revision suggested in brackets. Example:

> with whom
> **In his death cell, Joe Hill sent a letter to Big Bill Haywood, he had worked ~~with Haywood~~ in**
> ^
> **the early days of the IWW. [*Restructure the sentence;* see G6-d.]**

1. Joe Hill's final letter to Big Bill Haywood had only five sentences, it contained one line about his death, one admonition to Haywood, and three comments related to Hill's burial. [*Use a colon;* see G6-b.]

2. He commented briefly about his death he said, "I die like a true rebel." [*Restructure the sentence;* see G6-d.]

3. Hill said, "Don't waste time mourning for me, organize instead." [*Use a semicolon;* see G6-b.]

4. Hill, in prison in Utah, did not want to be buried in that state, he asked Haywood to haul his body into Wyoming, a hundred miles away. [*Use a coordinating conjunction;* see G6-a.]

5. Hill gave only one reason for requesting burial in Wyoming, he said, "I don't want to be found dead in Utah." [*Make two sentences;* see G6-c.]

6. On the night before his execution, he wrote a final poem, in it he made two requests. [*Restructure the sentence;* see G6-d.]

7. He wanted his body to be cremated, he wanted his ashes to be allowed to blow freely around the earth. [*Use a coordinating conjunction;* see G6-a.]

8. Here's how he said it in his poem,

   Let the merry breezes blow
   My dust to where some flowers grow.
   Perhaps some fading flower then
   Would come to life and bloom again. [*Use a colon;* see G6-b.]

9. Joe Hill was not a great poet, however, he was clever with rhymes. [*Use a semicolon;* see G6-b.]

10. Even in his will he managed to fit in a humorous rhyme,

    This is my last and final will.
    Good luck to all of you.
                  — Joe Hill [*Use a colon;* see G6-b.]

EXERCISE G6-4   Run-on sentences   Before working this exercise, read section G6 in
A Writer's Reference, Fifth Edition.

Revise each of the following run-on sentences in the way you think is most effective. Example:

Joe Hill was not buried in Utah; he was not buried in Wyoming either.
                                ∧

1. After Joe Hill's death, his body was sent to Chicago, a large auditorium was secured for the funeral services.

2. More than thirty thousand people overflowed the auditorium, they jammed the streets as they followed the funeral train to the cemetery.

3. Very few of these mourners knew Joe Hill personally, nevertheless, he was a true hero to them.

4. On that Thanksgiving Day of 1915, they knew that other people mourned him too they heard eulogies to him in nine different languages.

5. Those mourners and thousands like them sang his songs, because they did, Joe Hill's name lived on.

6. Hill's satirical, angry songs often had a surprising tenderness, it is no wonder that he was named poet laureate of the Wobbly movement.

7. In some ways, Joe Hill's death freed him, in other ways, he remains a prisoner.

8. Joe Hill did get part of his deathbed wish, his body was cremated.

9. He was cremated at the cemetery afterward his ashes were put in thirty envelopes and sent all over the world.

10. The IWW kept one envelope, the Department of Justice confiscated it in 1918 for use in a trial. Since the envelope was never returned, part of Joe Hill is still "in prison."

EXERCISE G6-5   Run-on sentences: Guided review

Revise each run-on sentence in the following paragraphs, using the method of revision suggested by the rule number in the margin (see section G6 of *A Writer's Reference,* Fifth Edition). The first sentence has been revised for you.

Although he
~~He~~ never calls them by name, John Steinbeck immortalizes the Wobblies in *The*   *G6-d*
Grapes of Wrath. The novel is about the life of the Joad family. The Joads have lost their
farm during the Depression, the family has come to California seeking work. There is   *G6-d*
no permanent work for anyone, moreover, the money earned by picking crops is not   *G6-b*
enough to feed the family.

Union organizers have talked to the workers about organizing and striking. Tom,
the oldest Joad son, has listened to them, however, he has not yet joined them. Tom is in   *G6-a*
hiding because he has accidentally killed a man in a fight. He spends all his daylight
hours alone, he has lots of time to think about his family's situation. Tom becomes   *G6-a*
convinced that life is unfair for his people, he decides to leave the family, find the union   *G6-d*
men, and work with them.

He is inarticulate when he tries to explain to Ma what he hopes to do he gropes for   *G6-c*
words to express his frustration and his hope. Ma asks him how she will know about
him, she worries that he might get killed and she would not know. Tom's reassurances   *G6-a*
are almost mystical: "Wherever they's a fight so hungry people can eat, I'll be there an'
when our folks eat the stuff they raise an' live in the houses they build, I'll be there."

If Tom had had a copy of the Wobblies' "little red song book," he could have found
less mystical words. Every copy of the book contained the Wobblies' Preamble, the first   *G6-d*
sentence in the Preamble was unmistakably clear "The working class and the employ-   *G6-b*
ing class have nothing in common." Tom would have understood those words he would   *G6-b*
have believed them too.

Unit review: Grammatical sentences (G1–G6)

Edit the following paragraphs to eliminate grammatical errors. Rule numbers in the margin refer to appropriate rules in sections G1–G6 of *A Writer's Reference,* Fifth Edition. First try to find and correct the error on your own. Then look up the rule if you need to. The first revision has been done for you.

        represent
  The fables of Aesop ~~represents~~ the Western root of fable, but there are two strong   *G1-a*

Eastern roots of fable also: the Panchatantra and the Jataka tales.

  The Panchatantra is a collection of stories designed to teach a first prince and his

brothers how to rule over a kingdom. (Until a tutor taught the first prince with these

stories, him and his brothers would never stay in the schoolroom. The boys listened   *G3-c*

eagerly to this new tutor who their father had found.) They are usually longer than   *G3-d, G3-b*

Western fables and have people as well as animals for characters. Their tone sounds

differently, too. Aesop's fables make gentle fun of people's foibles, Panchatantra fables   *G4-b, G6-b*

teach lessons in how to achieve and hold power. This difference is easily recognize in the   *G2-d*

moral to one of the Panchatantra fables: "Do not strike an enemy of iron with a fist of

flesh. Wait until your enemy is stranded at the bottom of a well. Then throw stones

upon him."

  The stories that carry the name "Jataka" tells about the Buddha and the adven-   *G1-a*

tures he had when he came to earth in various incarnations. In these stories, the Bud-

dha appeared as an animal. Or sometimes simply as a "wise old man." Like the   *G2-f, G5-b*

Panchatantra stories, the Jataka tales often depict people's foibles and shortcomings,

but the Jataka tales are not satiric. They promote compassion rather than power.

  In one story, for example, monkeys try to help their friend the gardener by water-

ing newly planted trees for him. In doing so, they pull each tree out of the ground to see

how long their roots are. Of course the trees die. The Buddha comments, "The ignorant   *G3-a*

and foolish, even when they desire to do good, often do ill."

  Putting all three traditions of fable together, any reader can choose from a rich

combination of small stories that carry large messages.

EXERCISE T1-1   Articles: Guided practice

Edit the following paragraphs to correct the use of articles. Rule numbers in the margin refer to appropriate rules in section T1 of *A Writer's Reference,* Fifth Edition. The first revision has been done for you, and a suggested revision of this exercise appears in the back of the book.

The
    United States has always attracted immigrants. Modern scientists think that first   *T1-d, T1-c*

immigrants arrived at least 25,000 years ago, probably traveling over land bridge just   *T1-a*

below the Arctic Circle — from Siberia to Alaska. (Of course land bridge is no longer   *T1-c*

there. Scientists think that such a bridge formed during the Ice Age, when much of

water in the ocean froze into tall glaciers. As it froze, it exposed large strips of land.   *T1-c*

Hunters probably followed animals across this land bridge.)

    Descendants of the original immigrants were still here in 1607 when settlers from

the England arrived in Virginia. These early settlers were followed by many more. In   *T1-d*

the hundred and forty years that followed, thousands made trip to America. Crowded   *T1-c*

onto small wooden boats, they left behind their kinfolk and their history and crossed

the Atlantic Ocean. Making such a trip took a bravery and faith in the future.   *T1-b*

    Some of the settlers came for religious reasons; others came to escape poverty or

imprisonment. But all of them came hoping for a happiness. They were followed by   *T1-b*

many others with same goal. Ever since those first immigrants 25,000 years ago, waves   *T1-c*

of the immigrants have continued to arrive on America's shores.   *T1-d*

EXERCISE T1-2   Articles   Before working this exercise, read section T1 in *A Writer's Reference,* Fifth Edition.

Some of the following sentences have errors in the use of articles. Mark the correct sentences "OK" and correct the others. Example:

>   *a*
> **European immigrants to America hoped for ~~an~~ friendly reception; some got quite a surpris-**
>   ^
> **ing welcome.**

1. In 1621, several Pilgrims were actually greeted by an Native American who spoke English and offered them a pleasant welcome.

2. Squanto was a member of the Pawtuxet tribe and became a real friend of the Pilgrims.

3. An explorer had taken Squanto to visit England in 1605; his visit there had turned into an lengthy one.

4. Squanto stayed in London almost a decade until a ship brought him back to America in 1614.

5. He had not been home very long when he was kidnapped and sent to Spain as slave, but he escaped and caught a ship to England.

6. In 1619, a English sea captain brought him back to a place Squanto knew, Cape Cod.

7. Squanto acted as useful interpreter and a unselfish guide for the Pilgrims.

8. The settlers wanted to grow a corn, but they had a hard time learning to farm in this new land.

9. Squanto gave the settlers an advice about planting their corn: He told them to plant a dead fish with each seed for fertilizer.

10. When Squanto died of a fever in 1622, Plymouth Colony lost an unsung hero who many historians believe was responsible for the success of the colony.

EXERCISE T1-3   Articles   Before working this exercise, read section T1 in *A Writer's Reference,* Fifth Edition.

Each of the following sentences has one missing or misused article. Correct each sentence. Example:

the
Not all newcomers to America have come for ʌ same reasons.

1. Whatever their reasons for coming, early immigrants to the America came of their own free will.

2. In the eighteenth and nineteenth centuries, hundreds of thousands of the Africans were brought to America by slave traders.

3. Slaves were sold primarily to southern farmers, who wanted a cheap labor.

4. Hundreds of thousands of Africans were brought to United States before 1861.

5. Each one was brought specifically to be an slave.

6. Some European immigrants came as indentured servants; they had borrowed cost of their voyage and had to work for their "owners" until the debt was repaid.

7. But these workers were promised the freedom after their debts had been paid.

8. The Africans had only hard work and the mistreatment.

9. Early settlers in America came primarily to North; slaves came primarily to the South.

10. America fought war to end slavery so that people would come to America only of their own free will.

EXERCISE T1-4   Articles: Guided review

Edit the following paragraphs to correct the use of articles. Rule numbers in the margin refer to appropriate rules in section T1 in *A Writer's Reference,* Fifth Edition. The first revision has been done for you.

the

One reason people immigrated to ⌃ United States was to escape poverty. Parents   *T1-d*

who could not earn enough money to take care of their children in their native land

tried to find other places to live. All during the nineteenth century, immigrants flocked

to America to escape a poverty. Unable in their own countries to provide for their fami-   *T1-b*

lies, they left their homes to seek their fortunes in a unknown land.   *T1-a*

Sometimes only one family member came to the new land. The father of the family

would come alone, hoping to earn enough money to send back for a mother and children.   *T1-c*

Other times, the whole family made the journey together to the other side of the Atlan-

tic. Irish and European families by the thousands settled on the East Coast of the United

States, often bringing only the clothes on their backs. It took a self-confidence to leave   *T1-b*

all that was familiar and start over again in new world. Self-confidence, hard work, and   *T1-a*

determination paid off for many immigrants. Before long, for example, the Irish were

movers and shakers in the politics.   *T1-d*

Norwegians and Swedes came to the East Coast also, but they kept moving until

they arrived in the Minnesota. Why did they decide to settle there? They were attracted   *T1-d*

by price of land in Minnesota: It was free. With their own labor, families could turn   *T1-c*

acres of prairie grasses into fields of corn and wheat. Families could raise enough food

for themselves and have enough left over to trade for other things or to sell for cash.

To families who had never owned land and were escaping from poverty, the United

States offered chance to start over. It offered them their best hope for a happiness.   *T1-a, T1-b*

EXERCISE T2-1   Special problems with verbs: Guided practice

Edit the following paragraphs to correct problems with verbs. Rule numbers in the margin refer to appropriate rules in section T2 of *A Writer's Reference,* Fifth Edition. The first revision has been done for you, and a suggested revision of this exercise appears in the back of the book.

            come
Immigrants have ~~came~~ to the United States from all over the world. Initially, new   *T2-a*

settlers were mostly European, Irish, or English. By the twentieth century, many Asians

had took the frightening boat trip across the Pacific. Usually the men came first. After   *T2-a*

they had made enough money for passage, their wives and children were bring over. All   *T2-a*

were in search of the same good life that earlier European immigrants had sought.

Unable to live comfortably in their homelands, a large number of Chinese and Japanese

gave up them and settled in the western part of the United States.   *T2-d*

These new immigrants worked on the railroads and in the mines. American busi-

nesses recruited Chinese labor because it was difficult to find American workers who

would accept the wages that were paying. Why did workers decided to come to America   *T2-a, T2-a*

anyway? Somehow the idea got started that America was a "golden mountain," where

people could pick up gold nuggets after an easy climb. Once they got here, most immi-

grants worked hard because they hoped making enough money to bring relatives over   *T2-c*

to America too.

Before and during World War II, many Germans who had been persecuted by Hitler

escaped to America. After the war, thousands of "displaced persons" were welcome by   *T2-a*

the United States. Later, refugees from Asia, Africa, Latin America, and the Caribbean

wanted being accepted. Franklin D. Roosevelt once said, "All of our people all over the   *T2-c*

country, except the pure-blooded Indians, are immigrants or descendants of immigrants."

If Roosevelt were alive today, he will know that his statement still true.   *T2-b, T2-e*

EXERCISE T2-2   Helping verbs and main verbs   Before working this exercise, read section T2 in *A Writer's Reference,* Fifth Edition.

A. Edit the italicized verb or verb phrase in each of the following sentences to correct the error in the use of helping verbs or main verbs. The revised verbs should all be in the passive voice. Example:

> In the early twentieth century, so many immigrants wanted to enter the United States that a
> special center *was ~~build~~* to process them.
>   *built*

1. That center, Ellis Island, *had built* to handle five thousand people a day, but often ten thousand people were processed in one day.

2. All immigrants *were check* by a doctor, and an immigrant's coat was marked with a code if a problem was suspected.

3. Everyone knew that if an immigrant *was gave* an "X," the immigrant had practically no chance to enter America; an "X" meant "possible mental problems."

4. Sometimes families were divided because one child was rejected for some reason; often the child *would sent* back alone.

5. Although it was the entrance to a new life for many people, "Ellis Island" *was translate* as "Isle of Tears" in many European languages.

B. Four of the following sentences have incorrect helping verbs or main verbs. Find and correct them. Mark "OK" next to the one correct sentence. Example:

> Where did most immigrants to the United States in the 1980s ~~came~~ from?
>   *come*

6. Eighty percent of the immigrants who were allow to come to the United States in the 1980s were Asian or Latin American.

7. The number of Asians who were lived in the United States more than doubled between 1970 and 1980.

8. People from the Philippines, China, and Korea been regular immigrants to the United States.

9. Since 1975, a rush of immigrant refugees been arriving in the United States.

10. In less than a seven-year period, 600,000 refugees from Vietnam, Laos, and Cambodia came to the United States.

EXERCISE T2-3   Helping verbs, main verbs, and omitted verbs   Before working this exercise, read section T2 in *A Writer's Reference,* Fifth Edition.

A. In the following sentences, underline the correct phrase in parentheses. Example:

(Haven't you hear, <u>Haven't you heard</u>) of Eckeo Kounlavong?

1. Eckeo Kounlavong (was born, had born) in Laos, lived in a refugee camp in Thailand, and now lives in Nashville, Tennessee.

2. Many people (do not knew, do not know) that in Laos, Eckeo was the leader of the Royal Laotian Classical Dance Troupe.

3. Before him, the troupe (had been directed, had been directing) by his father and grandfather.

4. In those days in Laos, the law said that the families of all the dancers (must living, must live) in the palace.

5. They (could not to dance, could not dance) for anyone except the king and his guests.

B. Four of the following sentences have omitted or incorrect helping verbs or main verbs. Find and correct them. Mark "OK" next to the one correct sentence. Example:

The dancers' lives were <u>~~change~~</u> drastically when the Communists gained power in Laos.
                              ^changed

6. Eckeo and his mother escaped from Laos to the Nongkhai refugee camp in Thailand.

7. The troupe was resettled in Nashville, Tennessee; they been in Nashville ever since.

8. Since 1980, Nashville has attract many Laotians.

9. Nashville has long been knowing as the country music capital of the United States.

10. Now Nashville can claims it is the capital for country music and for classical Laotian music.

EXERCISE T2-4   Helping verbs and main verbs Before working this exercise, read section T2 in *A Writer's Reference,* Fifth Edition.

Insert appropriate helping verbs in the following sentences. Sometimes two answers are possible. Example:

<u>Do (or Did)</u> **you know many musicians?**

1. Immigrants _____ brought much music to the United States.

2. _____ you heard of Seiji Ozawa, the former conductor of the Boston Symphony Orchestra?

3. _____ you know that he is from Japan?

4. Eileen Farrell, who _____ known internationally as a Metropolitan Opera star, is the daughter of the Irish "Singing O'Farrells."

5. Americans _____ been awed by Chinese cellist Yo-Yo Ma.

6. Chuing Chou, a Chinese American composer, _____ awarded a Guggenheim Fellowship.

7. Yi Knei Sze, a Chinese American singer, _____ won international fame.

8. _____ the name Myung Whun Chung mean anything to you?

9. Many critics think that this young Korean who studied at Juilliard _____ become one of America's outstanding pianists and composers.

10. Mischa Elman, Jascha Heifetz, and Nathan Milstein, all famous American violinists, _____ born in Russia and immigrated to the United States.

EXERCISE T2-5   Helping verbs and main verbs   Before working this exercise, read
section T2 in *A Writer's Reference,* Fifth Edition.

Turn each of the following sentence openings into a complete sentence using the correct main verb form. Choose from these verbs: *give, name, take, buy, offer.* Example:

I did not _take my children to the concert._ _____

1. Did you_____

2. He could not _____

3. An award was_____

4. She has already _____

5. They do _____

6. Immigrants have _____

7. Does your father _____

8. My uncle could _____

9. The house is _____

10. I have been _____

EXERCISE T2-6   Conditional verbs Before working this exercise, read section T2-b in *A Writer's Reference,* Fifth Edition.

Edit the following paragraph for problems with conditional verbs. The first revision has been made for you. You should make five more.

  If my grandfather had immigrated today, instead of eighty years ago, he probably ~~will~~ have *would*
traveled by jet. He came from Croatia to the United States just before the First World War. In those days, when you left your native country, you usually do so forever. My grandfather missed Croatia, but he liked America very much. He always said that America was a country where if you work hard, you would be successful. My grandfather, who will be ninety-five years old if he were alive today, was not as successful as he had hoped. If he has earned more money, he would have gone back to Croatia to visit. I'm sure my grandfather will have enjoyed that trip if he had ever had the chance to make it.

EXERCISE T2-7   Verbs followed by gerunds or infinitives   Before working this exercise, read section T2 in *A Writer's Reference,* Fifth Edition.

A. The gerunds and infinitives are italicized in the following sentences. Only one in each sentence is correct; correct the other one. Example:

> **Among the many Laotian refugees in Thailand's Nongkhai refugee camp were some members**
>   *to continue*
> **of the Royal Laotian Classical Dance Troupe. They wanted ~~continuing~~ their dancing and**
>   ^
> **discussed *finding* ways that they could stay together.**

1. In the refugee camp in Thailand, the dance troupe began *to think* about *to resettle* together.

2. They enjoyed *to work* together on their music and liked *to perform* for others.

3. Someone suggested *discussing* the idea with resettlement officials who might help them *staying* together.

4. The Laotians wanted *resettling* together; they suggested *sending* the 70 dancers and their families — 260 people — to one place.

5. They hardly dared *wishing* for that possibility; nevertheless, they enjoyed *thinking* about it.

B. Correct the use of gerunds and infinitives in the following sentences. Put "OK" next to the one correct sentence. Example:

>   *to come*
> **The United States allowed the Laotian dancers ~~coming~~ to America together.**
>   ^

6. The officials let them to bring all their equipment and costumes for performing in their new country.

7. Refugee officials needed to handle thousands of pieces of paper for the dancers before they finished to process them.

8. To avoid splitting up the troupe, officials asked resettlement agencies in America finding sponsors for all of the dancers and their families in one community.

9. People in Nashville, Tennessee, offered to let the troupe settle there.

10. The Laotians wanted thanking the people of Nashville by giving a concert for the city.

EXERCISE T2-8   Two-word verbs   Before working this exercise, read section T2 in *A Writer's Reference,* Fifth Edition.

A. Insert the correct two-word verb in each of the following sentences. A synonym for the verb is in parentheses at the end of each sentence. Choose from these two-word verbs: *help out, keep up, make up, put on, turn down.* Example:

Nashville _helped out_ the Laotians. (aided)

1. Laotians _____ much of Northern Telecom's work force. (constitute)

2. Telecom says that they are excellent employees and seldom _____ an opportunity for extra work. (reject)

3. They _____ their musical skill by practicing on weekends. (preserve)

4. They _____ special programs for cities in the area and for their cultural celebrations. (produce)

5. They _____ many of their cultural traditions this way. (maintain)

B. In each of the following sentences, underline the correct two-word verb. A synonym for the verb is in parentheses after the sentence. Example:

The dance troupe (<u>ran into</u>, ran out of) many difficulties. (encountered)

6. Trained as dancers, the troupe members had to (look over, look into) other ways to earn money when they settled in Nashville. (investigate)

7. Since they were the first Laotians in Nashville, they had no old friends whom they could (look over, look up, look into) in the city. (find, visit)

8. The new life in Nashville was difficult, but the Laotians did not (give up, give in) their dancing. (abandon)

9. They have (taken care of, taken off) their traditions while learning new American ones. (preserved)

10. No doubt their American friends will (pick out, pick up) some information about Laotian customs also. (learn)

EXERCISE T2-9 Special problems with verbs: Guided review

Edit the following paragraphs to correct errors in the use of verbs. Rule numbers in the margin refer to appropriate rules in section T2 of *A Writer's Reference,* Fifth Edition. The first sentence has been revised for you.

        Although most refugee immigrants have ~~adapt~~ *adapted* well to life in America, some have   *T2-a*

not. Many have great difficulty learning English and accepting the customs of this land

they have came to. Other newcomers find that they miss their former homes more than   *T2-a*

they thought they would. They believe that they would have been much happier if they

have stayed in their native countries. Among the Laotians, the saddest stories indicate   *T2-b*

that homesickness can even cause death. Would you believe that homesickness could be

so powerful? Young Laotian men with no apparent health problems have died suddenly

in their sleep. Doctors can to give no reason for these deaths, but Laotians believe that   *T2-a*

the young men wanted going home too much. They say that the young men gave to their   *T2-c*

feelings in, and their bodies died so that their spirits could enjoy to go home again.   *T2-d, T2-c*

        Immigrants from Mexico, Cuba, and Puerto Rico have had problems, too. Many

Mexican immigrants been forcibly repatriated because the American government con-   *T2-e*

sidered them "illegal" immigrants. Most Cuban immigrants in the 1960s expected their

stay in America to be temporary, so they did not became U.S. citizens. Because Puerto

Ricans are U.S. citizens, they are not really "immigrants." They here because they are   *T2-e*

looking for a better life. They do not always find it. So many Puerto Ricans have re-

turned to their homeland that they have been give a special name, "Neoricans."   *T2-a*

        Most immigrants, however, have adapt to the new country, changing themselves —   *T2-a*

and it.

EXERCISE T3/T4-1   Sentence structure and other trouble spots: Guided practice

Edit the following paragraphs to correct any misuses of subjects, expletives, adjectives, adverbs, participles, and prepositions. Rule numbers in the margin refer to appropriate rules in sections T3 and T4 of *A Writer's Reference,* Fifth Edition. The first revision has been done for you, and a suggested revision of this exercise appears in the back of this book.

A descendant of early immigrants ~~at~~ to North America played a pivotal role in help-   *T4-b*

ing later Americans explore their country. Were tribes of American Indians living all   *T3-a*

over what is now the United States. Each tribe had its own language and customs.

Some tribes raided others and took prisoners who then became the raiding tribes' slaves.

That is what happened to a young Shoshone girl now known as Sacagawea.

This girl, like many young Shoshones, she had a nickname, "He-toe." "He-toe" was   *T3-b*

the sound a local bird made, and the girl's movements were so swift that friends thought

she resembled that bird. When a raiding party of Hidatsas captured easily this young   *T3-e*

girl, they named her Sacagawea — "bird woman." The frightening young girl did not try   *T4-a*

to escape but accepted her role and worked for her captors. At a few months, she had   *T4-b*

acquired a reputation for good sense and good work.

The tribe married Sacagawea to a white man, Toussaint Charbonneau; she was his

second wife. Soon pregnant, this typical Indian wife she did the chores and left all deci-   *T3-b*

sions to her husband; but inwardly, she longed to explore new places and meet new

people. She may have been controlling by her husband, but she never missed a chance   *T4-a*

to learn whatever she could.

When white men appeared, all the Indians were curious. Sacagawea had never

seen a man with yellow hair — or red hair. Nor had she ever seen a black man. All these

men were trying to get to the "Big Water" far to the west. They would have to cross

mountains that they had not even seen them yet. They needed horses, guides, and an   *T3-c*

interpreter who could speak the Shoshone language. Imagine their surprise when this

interpreter, whom they had hoped to find him, turned out to be a woman — a Shoshone,   *T3-c*

young, attractive woman.   *T3-e*

EXERCISE T3/T4-2 Omissions and needless repetitions Before working this exercise, read sections T3 and T4 in *A Writer's Reference,* Fifth Edition.

In the following sentences, add needed subjects or expletives and delete any repeated subjects, objects, or adverbs. Mark the two correct sentences "OK." Example:

> **The white men who came ashore ~~they~~ had been sent by the Great White Father in Washington to blaze a trail to the Big Water.**

1. The two leaders among the white men they were Meriwether Lewis and William Clark.

2. Clark's red beard and hair puzzled Sacagawea; was hard to believe that those red hairs were real.

3. Sacagawea also watched in amazement as York, the black man, he washed his hands and face and none of his color came off.

4. The men quickly began building the shelters that they were going to live in them.

5. Was a lot of noise as they felled trees and fitted the logs together to build cabins.

6. The white men hired Charbonneau as an interpreter (he spoke both Hidatsa and French) and told him to bring Sacagawea along too.

7. Sacagawea could hardly believe that she would see her own people again in the place where she had lived there before.

8. Charbonneau and Sacagawea, who was now very large with child, were given a cabin to live in that winter.

9. Sacagawea's friends came often to the house that she was staying in it, usually asking for medical help while they were there.

10. Sacagawea, who learned how to cook for these men, she tried especially to please Captain Clark, who gave her an English name, Janie.

EXERCISE T3/T4-3   Placement of adjectives   Before working this exercise, read sections T3 and T4 in *A Writer's Reference,* Fifth Edition.

Insert the adjectives into their correct positions in the following sentences. Do not add commas. Example:

> **old, experienced**
>
> <u>Experienced</u> <u>old</u>   **women came to help Sacagawea when it was time for her baby to be born.**

1. log, warm

   Sacagawea was glad that she was living in a _____ _____ cabin when birthing time came.

2. hard, labor

   The baby did not come easily. Neither the old women's skill nor Captain Clark's medicines did much to ease Sacagawea's _____ _____ pains.

3. old, the, bell-shaped

   Finally, one of the men said that swallowing some rattles (_____ _____ _____ scales on a rattlesnake's tail) often brought a quick and easy birth.

4. dark, strange, this

   Captain Clark had collected some rattles; he crushed two of them and added some water. One of the old women gave _____ _____ _____ potion to Sacagawea.

5. male, a, healthy

   Ten minutes later, Jean Baptiste Charbonneau arrived — _____ _____ _____ child who would be affectionately called "Pomp," the Shoshone word for "first born."

EXERCISE T3/T4-4   **Use of present and past participles**   Before working this exercise, read sections T3 and T4 in *A Writer's Reference,* Fifth Edition.

Circle the letter of the sentence that answers the question. Example:

In which sentence were the men eager to get started?

a. By April, the snows were melting and the men in the camp were exciting.

b. By April, the snows were melting and the men in the camp were excited.

1. In which sentence were the men happy?

    a. Sacagawea always found the men pleasing.

    b. Sacagawea always found the men pleased.

2. In which sentence was Sacagawea herself eager to get there?

    a. As they neared the mountains, Sacagawea grew more and more excited.

    b. As they neared the mountains, Sacagawea grew more and more exciting.

3. In which sentence did Clark enjoy watching Sacagawea?

    a. Watching Sacagawea bargain for horses, Clark was fascinating.

    b. Watching Sacagawea bargain for horses, Clark was fascinated.

4. In which sentence were the travelers unhappy?

    a. For the four months they stayed on the West Coast, the travelers had only twelve days without rain; all of them found this weather depressed.

    b. For the four months they stayed on the West Coast, the travelers had only twelve days without rain; all of them found this weather depressing.

5. In which sentence did Lewis and Clark make Sacagawea fearful?

    a. On the way home, Lewis and Clark made a frightened decision to divide the crew and send the men along different trails.

    b. On the way home, Lewis and Clark made a frightening decision to divide the crew and send the men along different trails.

EXERCISE T3/T4-5   Sentence structure and other trouble spots: Guided review

Edit the following paragraphs to correct any misuses of subjects, expletives, adjectives, adverbs, participles, and prepositions. Do not change correct sentences. Rule numbers in the margin refer to appropriate rules in sections T3 and T4 of *A Writer's Reference,* Fifth Edition. The first revision has been done for you.

By the time Lewis and Clark ~~found~~ |finally| the Pacific Ocean and made their way   *T3-e*

home again, Sacagawea had not only gotten her wish to travel, but this Shoshone young   *T3-e*

woman had also become a favorite of all the crew. Had served as interpreter, guide, cook,   *T3-a*

nurse, and mother for everyone who needed her. She and Pomp seemed like family to

Clark and his men.

When Captain Clark left, he offered to take Pomp (now almost two) to St. Louis

and educate him. Sacagawea said, "Not now," but later the whole family moved in St.   *T4-b*

Louis. No one is sure what happened next. Most historians agree that after a few months

Charbonneau left gladly St. Louis "with his wife" and spent time at a new fort, Fort   *T3-e*

Manuel, where his wife she sickened and died of a fever in 1812. Since Charbonneau   *T3-b*

had several Shoshone wives, cannot be sure that this wife was Sacagawea. Historical   *T3-a*

records show that Clark became the legal guardian for Pomp and his baby sister the

year that Charbonneau's wife died.

Pomp stayed with Captain Clark. At nineteen, he met a German prince who was

touring America and went to Europe with him for six years. Later this mountain man,

whose mother had trekked with him halfway across the continent before he could walk,

he returned to mountain life for good, working as a trader, hunter, and interpreter.   *T3-b*

The Shoshone oral tradition says that Sacagawea quarreled with Charbonneau and

left him, stayed for a while with the Comanches, met up with her son and a nephew, and

ended up at the Wind River Reservation in Wyoming, where she died on April 4, 1884,

almost one hundred years old. The Wyoming branch of the Daughters of the American

Revolution were convincing that the oral tradition was true and erected a memorial   *T4-a*

stone there.

No other American woman has had so many memorials dedicated to her. Among them are historical markers, lakes, a river, a mountain peak, and a park. Then, on 1999, the United States minted a new dollar — a gold-colored coin. Just below the word "Liberty" on that coin is a likeness of Sacagawea with her infant son. Sacagawea, who loved travel, will now go hundreds of new places where Americans take her there in their purses and pockets.

T4-b

T3-c

Unit review: Editing for ESL problems (T1–T4)

This paragraph has eleven errors. Rule numbers in the margin refer to appropriate rules in sections T1–T4 of *A Writer's Reference,* Fifth Edition. The first revision has been done for you. Find and correct ten more errors.

      Immigrants have ~~gave~~ *given* the United States their language, their foods, and their   *T2-a*

customs. Native Americans gave the United States the names for half of its states.

"Texas" is an Indian old word for "friends," and "Idaho" means "good morning." Spanish   *T3-e*

immigrants gave the United States the longest name for any of its cities. In Spanish, is   *T3-a*

El Pueblo de Nuestra Señora la Reina de los Angeles de Porciúncula — Los Angeles.

American cuisine now includes foods of many other traditions, from Chinese sweet-

and-sour pork to Greek baklava. American children who enjoy to eat pizza or spaghetti   *T2-c*

or tacos think they are eating American food. Since the Germans brought the Christ-

mas tree to America, every immigrant group that celebrates Christmas it has added   *T3-b*

something to American Christmas customs. Fiestas and serenades are common in the

United States, and even New England children often want breaking a piñata on their   *T2-c, T4-b*

birthday parties. Every summer in Washington, D.C., Americans celebrate the diversity

of their culture with an excited folk festival. Groups from many different cultures in   *T4-a*

America bring an equipment to produce their own foods and festivities on the national   *T1-b*

Mall, where many other Americans can enjoy them. A alien visitor from Mars would not   *T1-a*

be able to tell which songs and stories are "American," for the food, festivals, dances,

music, and folktales of immigrant groups have became part of America's own culture.   *T2-a*

EXERCISE P1/P2-1   The comma: Guided practice

Edit the following essay by adding commas where they are needed and removing unnecessary commas. Rule numbers in the margin refer to appropriate rules in sections P1 and P2 of *A Writer's Reference*, Fifth Edition. The first revision has been made for you, and answers to this exercise appear in the back of the book.

If a boy wanted to join the football team at Carlisle Indian School, he had to go   *P1-b*
through a difficult test. Any boy who wanted to be on the team had to stand at one of the
goal lines; all the first-string players stood around the field. When the ball was punted
to the new boy, he had to catch it and try to get all the way to the other end zone with it.
The team members tried to stop him before he could get very far. Only a few players had
ever gotten as far as the fifty-yard line so "Pop" Warner, coach at the Carlisle Indian   *P1-a*
School considered it a good test.   *P1-e*

One day a quiet Indian boy surprised Pop. The boy caught the ball, started running, wheeled away from the first players who tried to stop him, shook off the
others and ran the ball all the way to the opposite goal line. Convinced that the player's   *P1-c*
success was an accident, the coach ordered him to run the play again. Brusquely, the
coach spoke to the players, and reminded them that this workout was supposed to be   *P2-a*
tackling practice. Jim, the nineteen-year-old six-footer, simply said "Nobody tackles Jim."   *P1-h*
Then he ran the ball to the goal line a second time.

Well, almost no one tackled Jim Thorpe successfully for many years. Life itself got
him down and made him fumble more often than his football opponents did, but, he was   *P2-g*
usually able to recover and go on. The first blow was the death of his twin brother while
the two boys were still in grade school. This tragedy was followed by others; by the time
Jim was twenty-five, he had lost his brother, his mother, and his father to death. They
left him a Native American heritage: His father was half Irish and half Native American and his mother was the granddaughter of a famous, Indian warrior named Chief   *P1-a, P2-d*
Black Hawk.

Fortunately or unfortunately, along with his Native American heritage came great
pride and stoicism. That pride kept him silent when the greatest blow of all came: He

was forced to return the Olympic medals he had won in 1912 because he was declared to be not an amateur. He dealt stoically with his personal tragedies. When infantile paralysis struck his son Jim Thorpe disappeared for a few days to deal with the tragedy alone. His stoicism also saw him through a demotion to the minor leagues and sad years of unemployment and poverty before his death.

P1-b

Even death's tackle may not have been totally successful: After Jim Thorpe's death his Olympic medals were returned, and a town was named after him.

P1-b

EXERCISE P1/P2-2   **The comma**   Before working this exercise, read sections P1 and P2 in *A Writer's Reference,* Fifth Edition.

A. Insert commas where they are needed with coordinating conjunctions in the following sentences. If a sentence is correct, mark it "OK." Example:

> **Coach Warner was impressed with the new player's skill, and he looked for a chance to try him in an actual game.**

1. Jim passed Coach Warner's test but he did not get to play right away.

2. Then in one game a player was injured and Coach Warner sent Jim in.

3. At first no one but Jim and the coach believed Jim could play well enough.

4. He lost five yards the first time he got the ball but the next time he ran sixty-five yards for a touchdown.

5. His sports career began with that game and included major honors in track, lacrosse, baseball, and football.

B. Insert commas when they are needed after an introductory element, in a series, and with coordinate adjectives. If a sentence is correct, mark it "OK." Example:

> **After trying to tackle Thorpe only once, Jim's most famous opponent never played football again.**

6. In a game against Army, Carlisle's Thorpe had the ball.

7. One Army player tried to tackle Jim, failed, injured his knee in the process and had to be helped from the field. OK

8. That strong confident player said in later years, "Thorpe gained ground; he *always* gained ground."

9. Although the injured player was never able to play football again he became famous in other ways.

10. He became supreme commander of the Allied armies in Europe in World War II and thirty-fourth president of the United States — Dwight D. Eisenhower.
OK

EXERCISE P1/P2-3 **The comma** Before working this exercise, read sections P1 and P2 in *A Writer's Reference,* Fifth Edition.

A. Add commas where needed around nonrestrictive elements. If a sentence is correct, mark it "OK." Example:

> **Jim Thorpe's Olympic medals, which he won in 1912 but had to forfeit, were for the pentath-lon and the decathlon. [*Thorpe won Olympic medals only in 1912.*]**

1. The Carlisle students who needed summer jobs, often played baseball for Carolina teams. [*Not all Carlisle students needed summer jobs.*]

2. The players who were willing to lie used false names, when they played for little-known teams; Jim did not. [*Only some of the players were willing to lie.*]

3. Those who had received money for playing their sport were disqualified because they were no longer "amateurs." [*Only some competitors received money.*] OK

4. The five-sport event, which is called the pentathlon is difficult. [*There is only one five-sport event.*]

5. The decathlon which is a ten-sport event, is considered the most difficult of all Olympic events. [*There is only one ten-sport event.*]

B. Add commas as necessary in the following sentences. Example:

> **In Stockholm, Sweden's King Gustav presented the 1912 Olympic winners with their gold medals; in addition, he spoke briefly to some of them.**

6. As King Gustav presented Jim Thorpe's 1912 Olympic medal, he said to Jim "Sir you are the greatest athlete in the world."

7. In January 1913, however, a newspaper reported that Jim had been paid for playing for the Carolina baseball teams.

8. When the Amateur Athletic Union (AAU), asked Jim said he had been paid.

9. Stating that he had not known he was doing wrong, Jim insisted that he had acted no worse than athletes who used false names. OK

10. Jim having presented his case, the AAU made its ruling; specifically it ruled that Jim had not been an amateur at the time of the Olympics. OK

EXERCISE P1/P2-4 **The comma** Before working this exercise, read sections P1 and P2 in *A Writer's Reference,* Fifth Edition.

Edit the following paragraphs to correct the use of commas. The first revision has been done for you. You should add ten more commas.

When the Amateur Athletic Union ruled that 1912 Olympic winner Jim Thorpe had not been an amateur at the time he won his medals, several consequences followed. Once the ruling was formally stated, Jim Thorpe's name was erased from the Olympic records. In addition he had to return his medals. Friends wanted him to fight the AAU ruling but he was too proud to do so.

During the next sixteen years that Jim played football was quite different from what it is today. Players then had no league, no formal schedule, no required helmets and often no salaries. Then representatives of eight concerned teams met to form a league. The organization they formed which was called the American Professional Football Association later became the National Football League; Jim Thorpe was its first president.

Jim's playing declined with the years until on November 30, 1929 an Associated Press story described him as "a mere shadow of his former self." No longer able to play sports Thorpe had to dig ditches in the Depression years. When the 1932 Olympics were held in Los Angeles California he could not afford to buy a ticket.

EXERCISE P1/P2-5   **The comma**   Before working this exercise, read sections P1 and
P2 in *A Writer's Reference,* Fifth Edition.

Each of the following sentences has one unnecessary comma. Delete the comma that is not needed.
Example:

> **Along with other bad news about Thorpe, newspaper stories reported/ that he drank too**
> **much and that drinking caused his second marriage to go wrong.**

1. After Jim Thorpe's death, his friends still worked to have his medals restored, and to get his
   name back on the list of Olympic winners.

2. Knowing they would not be happy, until the AAU and the Olympic committees changed their
   minds, his friends made repeated appeals.

3. The AAU acted first, reversing itself some years later, (in 1973) by saying that Thorpe's titles
   should be restored.

4. The American Olympic Committee agreed two years later, but, it was not until 1982 that the
   International Olympic Committee voted to restore Jim's titles.

5. New, Olympic medals were presented to Thorpe's children in a 1983 ceremony in Los Angeles,
   California.

6. However, the International Olympic Committee, did not erase the names of the second-place
   finishers.

7. Even though Thorpe had beaten the other "winners," his friends had to accept the fact, that Jim
   would be listed only as a cochampion.

8. In the hearts of Jim's supporters remains the honest, firm conviction, that Jim should be listed
   as the sole winner.

9. They thought that the International Olympic Committee's reversing its position, restoring the
   titles, and awarding Thorpe's medals to his children, were not enough.

10. It is not likely that there will be any further action, such as, erasing the other winners' names.

EXERCISE P1/P2-6 **The comma** Before working this exercise, read sections P1 and
P2 in *A Writer's Reference,* Fifth Edition.

One sentence in each of the following pairs is correctly punctuated. Circle the letter of the correct
sentence and add or delete commas in the other one. Example:

(a.)**Jim Thorpe was a greater athlete than any other athlete of his time.**

b. **In 1950, an Associated Press poll of hundreds of sportswriters indicated that Thorpe was**
better/than any other athlete from 1900 to 1950.

1a. According to many experts, (sportswriters, coaches, and the like), Thorpe was the best athlete
in the entire twentieth century.

b. Others think that modern knowledge of various aspects of training (nutrition, drugs, and the
like) will produce even greater players in the future.

2a. People said, that Thorpe's confidence in himself was so great, that he often skipped practice at
the Olympics, and they told the "broad jump story," to illustrate his confidence.

b. Observers said that he measured the broad jump distance with his eye, decided he could jump
it, and lay down in a hammock for a nap, not even bothering to take a practice run at it.

3a. In his 289 games in baseball's major leagues, the only statistic that suggested trouble was his
batting average of .252.

b. It seems that the only thing, that really bothered Jim, was hitting curveballs.

4a. He had a peculiar style of running, that left his football tacklers flat on the ground.

b. He would twist his hips away from the player who was after him.

5a. He would wait until that player's head was at the exact, dangerous, height.

b. Then he would swing his hips with full, direct force right into the player's head.

EXERCISE P1/P2-7   The comma: Guided review

Edit the following paragraphs by adding commas where they are needed and removing commas where they are not needed. Rule numbers in the margin refer to appropriate rules in sections P1 and P2 in *A Writer's Reference,* Fifth Edition. The first revision has been done for you.

Quarrels about one of America's greatest athletes, Jim Thorpe, continue. Even though the decision about his Olympic standing has been made, other quarrels about him remain.

P1-b

After Jim Thorpe died his wife had to choose a burial place. Everyone assumed he would be buried in his home state of Oklahoma, but, his wife made other arrangements. Some people from Mauch Chunk, Pennsylvania, made her an offer. They said, that they wanted Jim buried in their town. Having his body there would make more tourists want to come to their small, Pennsylvania town. They talked of a burial place, a Jim Thorpe Museum and a hospital in his memory. They also offered to change the name of the town from Mauch Chunk to Jim Thorpe.

P1-b

P2-g

P2-g

P2-d

P1-c

Mrs. Thorpe, who wanted a memorial for Jim, agreed to these proposals, and gave Jim's body to the town. It is probable that at the core of her decision was the desire for Jim Thorpe to be remembered. After some negotiation, the agreement was concluded and the town is now on the map as "Jim Thorpe."

P2-a

P1-a

Jim's wife, not his children, made the agreement. His children, seven sons and daughters, wanted his body buried in Oklahoma. They wanted the body to be given a traditional Indian burial. They wanted the town to give back their father's body. Jack Thorpe, one of the sons, said to a *Sport Illustrated* writer in 1982 "Dad's spirit is still roaming." In Jim Thorpe's family pride is still part of the Thorpe heritage. The family has not given up the struggle. Other people have also asked the townspeople to change their minds.

P1-h

P1-b

Jim Thorpe lived a tough, honest, gifted, and controversial, life. Even if his records are someday broken, he will remain a legend of the American sports world.

P2-c

EXERCISE P3-1   The semicolon: Guided practice

Edit the following paragraphs for semicolon use. Rule numbers in the margin refer to appropriate rules in section P3 of *A Writer's Reference,* Fifth Edition. The first revision has been done for you, and answers to this exercise appear in the back of this book.

When Cheryl Toussaint came in second in a race she had never planned to run, *P3-d* she started on a road that led to the Olympics and a world record.

Cheryl began running almost by accident one day when she went to watch a city-sponsored track meet in Brooklyn, New York. During the preliminaries, the officials announced an "open" race, it was one that anyone could enter. Cheryl wanted to *P3-a* enter; but she was dressed in a skirt and sandals. Four things made her run; one friend *P3-d, P3-d* traded shoes with her, another let her borrow jeans, several called her "chicken" if she didn't run, and one girl dared her to run. Coming in second in that race led this teen-ager to many places, including Munich, Germany, Toronto, Canada, and Montreal, *P3-c* Canada.

There were, however, many races to run and lessons to learn. Cheryl joined the all-female Atoms Track Club, and she began training under Coach Fred Thompson. Like most coaches, Fred had his own way of testing newcomers. He watched a new runner carefully, however, he gave her no special attention. Instead, he just gave her orders one *P3-b* after another. He would tell Cheryl to run laps, go through exercises, and do practice starts, at the same time he would never comment on how she performed. If *P3-a* the newcomer endured the hard, time-consuming workouts without encouragement or praise; Thompson was sure that she was ready for real coaching. *P3-d*

Cheryl quit after two months, for six more months she stayed out. During that *P3-a* time she thought about her attitude toward work, her poor record at school, her pleasure in running, and her lack of goals. When she returned; Thompson welcomed her *P3-d* back. Coach Thompson knew how special Cheryl was, he not only convinced her she was *P3-a* college material but pushed her to achieve the highest goal of the amateur athlete — the Olympics.

EXERCISE P3-2   The semicolon   Before working this exercise, read section P3 in *A Writer's Reference,* Fifth Edition.

Add semicolons in the five word groups that need them; mark the other word groups "OK." Example:

> **Cheryl Toussaint's first run was an indication of her character and determination; no one could find fault with her effort.**

1. Cheryl's first run — at a cross-country meet on Long Island — would certainly have impressed any coach every person watching was astounded by her perseverance.

2. Coach Thompson had warned her not to start too fast but to stay with the pack. "Just try to finish," he said.

3. Too excited to follow his directions, Cheryl took off at top speed at the starting gun, moreover, she did not slow down even after she was a hundred yards in front of everyone else.

4. Cheryl kept that distance for most of the run, she did not allow herself any slack.

5. Then, with only a hundred yards to go, Cheryl gave out, she collapsed and fell down.

6. Immediately, she got to her knees and started crawling. She crawled toward the finish line, not to the grassy area where runners who left the race were supposed to go.

7. She got up, staggered a little farther, and fell again. Once more she started crawling.

8. Not able to get to her feet, Cheryl continued to crawl, after all, she was nearly to the finish line.

9. She had almost reached the line when another runner passed her and won.

10. "I knew at that moment," said her coach, "that this girl was going to be something special." Her coach was right.

EXERCISE P3-3   The semicolon   Before working this exercise, read section P3 in *A Writer's Reference,* Fifth Edition.

Each of the following sentences has two semicolons but should have only one. Delete the incorrect one and replace it with other punctuation if necessary. Example:

> **No one else had ever seen anything special in Cheryl, who had never shown any ambition; her teachers had labeled her a "slow learner" long before she got to high school.**

1. Cheryl had to beg her teachers to allow her to take college preparatory courses; they were sure she would fail; no matter how hard she tried.

2. Coach Thompson did many things for Cheryl; including coaching track, prodding her about schoolwork, encouraging good eating habits, and insisting that she think about college; most important of all, he gave her faith in herself.

3. All of the runners knew that if they made qualifying times; Coach Thompson would see to it that they were entered in the national meets; however, they also knew that if they did not qualify, they were off the team.

4. Cheryl soon discovered that she had to schedule her time; or she would fail at school or at track or at both; thinking about Coach Thompson, she began to care.

5. By the time Cheryl graduated from high school, she was an A student; this "slow learner" received an academic scholarship to New York University; although she had thought only an athletic one was possible.

EXERCISE P3-4   The semicolon: Guided review

Edit the following paragraphs for semicolon use. Rule numbers in the margin refer to appropriate rules in section P3 of *A Writer's Reference,* Fifth Edition. The first revision has been done for you.

Every runner dreams of winning both individual and relay medals at the Olympics/; in 1972, Cheryl Toussaint was no exception. When she did not make the individual finals; she pinned her hopes on the relay race. Her teammates on the American team were ready: Mabel Ferguson, Madeline Jackson, and Kathy Hammond. The relay was Cheryl's last chance to win a medal, unfortunately, it seemed that everything was against her.

P3-a

P3-d

P3-b

Cheryl began the third leg of the qualifying heat with runners ahead of her. Then a runner in front of her fell. As Cheryl dashed around her, another runner stepped on the heel of Cheryl's left shoe so Cheryl was running with her shoe half on and half off. She needed to stop and pull the shoe on; but she knew two things: She would lose valuable time, and this was her team's last chance to qualify for the finals. She kept running, very soon the shoe flew up in the air. Cheryl wondered whether the shoe would hit anyone, whether TV viewers could see her bare foot, and whether people in the stands had noticed. But she ran on, passing the other runners. Her team qualified for the finals that day, and in the finals, Cheryl and her teammates won silver medals.

P3-a

Cheryl remembered her very first run, at which she hadn't even known how to start, her first "real" race, at which she'd crawled to the finish line, and her most recent one, at which she'd failed to qualify for the 800-meter run. She could laugh about all those memories now, for she and her teammates were Olympic winners.

P3-c

Back home, Cheryl kept to her plans: graduating from college (with a B+ average), getting a job in the Federal Reserve Bank's management training program, and starting to train for the next Olympics. She knew that nothing would ever mean as much to her again as track, the Atoms, and Coach Thompson had meant her success was also theirs.

P3-a

EXERCISE P4-1   The colon: Guided practice

In the following paragraph, insert colons where they are needed, and eliminate any improperly used colons. Rule numbers in the margin refer to appropriate rules in section P4 of *A Writer's Reference*, Fifth Edition. The first revision has been done for you, and answers to this exercise appear in the back of this book.

In 1951, Althea Gibson broke the color barrier in women's tennis and became admired all over the world. No one who knew her as a teenager would have predicted her success. By the time Althea Gibson reached her teens, her record showed three indications of trouble: running away from home, dropping out of school, and losing the one job   *P4-a*

she had been able to find. To survive in her neighborhood, Althea depended on: a small welfare allowance, occasional handouts, and plain old luck. She listed her   *P4-d*

skills as the following, good bowler, great two-on-two basketball player, and fast   *P4-a*

paddleball player. Even after she began playing tennis and moving in upper-class Harlem society, she resented the efforts of the society ladies to improve her. They busied themselves with tasks such as: correcting her manners and restricting her behavior. Looking   *P4-d*

back, she later summed up her attitude she said she wasn't ready to study about "how   *P4-b*

to be a fine lady." At eighteen, she finally got: a waitress job, a congenial roommate, and   *P4-d*

a good friend.

EXERCISE P4-2 **The colon** Before working this exercise, read section P4 in *A Writer's Reference,* Fifth Edition.

In the following sentences, insert colons where they can be effectively used. Example:

In 1957, Althea Gibson won the women's title at the most prestigious tennis tournament in the world: Wimbledon.

1. Althea Gibson broke the color barrier in women's tennis she was the first black female player to compete in national championships.

2. Two tennis-playing doctors opened their homes to her so she could finish high school and go to college Dr. Hubert A. Eaton of Wilmington, North Carolina, and Dr. Robert W. Johnson of Lynchburg, Virginia.

3. Her life in a southern high school was not pleasant; if she had written a book about it, she could have titled it *Misfit, A Yankee Woman in a Southern School.*

4. Besides tennis, Althea's other love was music the drums, the chorus, and especially the saxophone.

5. Her friend Sugar Ray Robinson advised her firmly to go to college "No matter what you want to do, tennis or music or what, you'll be better at it if you get some education."

EXERCISE P4-3 The colon   Before working this exercise, read section P4 in *A Writer's Reference*, Fifth Edition.

In the following paragraphs, the italicized words indicate where two parts of a sentence come together. Decide whether the sentence needs a colon to join these parts. If so, insert it. If not, mark the spot "OK." The first spot has been done for you. HINT: You will need very few colons.

                                        OK

Althea Gibson began playing *tennis when* she was a young teenager in the 1940s. In just over a decade, she *became one* of the world's greatest women tennis players.

The tennis world began to notice her after only a few years of amateur *play she* was winning women's singles meets one after the other. In 1950 and the years immediately *following, she* became more and more famous. By 1957–58, Althea Gibson, the rising young tennis star, was well known on both sides of the *Atlantic she* was the most respected woman player in Britain and America. In both countries she won the national women's singles title two years in a row: 1957 and 1958. The British meet, which is *called the* Wimbledon, is generally regarded *as the* unofficial world championship meet. Gibson also played on the U.S. team at other major meets, *including the* Wightman Cup meet. That meet is a special British-American *meet that* pits U.S. women against British women. When Althea Gibson was on the U.S. team, the United States won.

Gibson's retirement from tennis in 1958 *was a* complete surprise to her fans. What reason did she give for her retirement? She had *decided to* become a professional golfer!

EXERCISE P4-4   The colon: Guided review

In the following paragraph, insert colons where they are needed and eliminate any improperly used colons. Rule numbers in the margin refer to appropriate rules in section P4 in *A Writer's Reference,* Fifth Edition. The first revision has been done for you.

When the Eatons of North Carolina invited Althea Gibson to move into their home for the school year, she hesitated. Northerner Althea had one major fear/: white   *P4-a* southerners. She decided to go in spite of her fears. At the Eatons' house, Althea had to get used to: wearing skirts, obeying rules, and getting along with people. She was ex-   *P4-d* pected to listen to adult conversations and join in with well-chosen comments. At the time, Althea considered these requirements to be serious disadvantages. However, there were also advantages to life at the Eatons, such as: regular meals, a room of her own, an   *P4-d* allowance, and unlimited use of the doctor's private tennis court. School presented one overwhelming social problem Althea could not make friends with either boys or girls.   *P4-b* The boys may have resented her athletic prowess and her self-confidence. The girls considered her a tomboy. Years later Althea still recalled their taunts "She's no lady"   *P4-a* and "Look at her throwing that ball just like a man." Even the singing instructor added to her woes. When he placed her in the tenor section to make the chorus sound better, the other girls in the chorus could not control their giggles. Some people even made fun of her tennis, but her tenacity paid off. Before she had finished high school, Florida A & M University had offered her a scholarship. Althea had been right to expect problems if she lived in the South, but she had not anticipated what the problems would be. If she had put those high school years into a book, she could have titled it *The Unexpected,*   *P4-c* *Problems Are Not Always What They Seem.*

EXERCISE P5-1   The apostrophe: Guided practice

In the following paragraphs, add apostrophes where they are missing, and delete or correct them where they have been misused. Rule numbers in the margin refer to appropriate rules in section P5 of *A Writer's Reference,* Fifth Edition. The first revision has been done for you, and answers to this exercise appear in the back of this book.

During the 1990 troubles in Panama, American television and newspaper reporters had an exciting piece of news. They reported that for the first time American female
soldiers had been engaged in actual combat. Acting as her ~~soldiers~~ *soldiers'* leader, Captain Linda   *P5-a*
Bray led her troops into combat. Names of two additional women who were involved in
combat, Staff Sergeant April Hanley and PFC Christina Proctor, were reported in the
newspapers. Their's were the only names reported, although other women also took   *P5-e*
part.

It was'nt the first time an American woman had fought in an American battle, but   *P5-c*
its not likely that many people are aware of that fact. The Civil War had its female   *P5-c*
fighters too. Loreta Janeta Velazquez fought for the Confederates' in the Civil War after   *P5-e*
her husbands death. Like many other women whose husbands were killed in that war,   *P5-a*
she must have asked herself, "Whose going to take his place in battle?" The decision to   *P5-c*
fight was hers alone. Someone is sure to ask how that was possible, even in those days.
Military I.D.s were not very sophisticated in the 1860s. Someones willingness to fight   *P5-b*
was that person's major qualification, and each fighting unit needed to replace it's losses   *P5-e*
as fast as possible. Velazquez simply disguised herself in mens clothing, found a troop   *P5-a*
needing replacements, and joined the fight. Loreta Janeta Velazquez was Linda Brays   *P5-a*
Civil War predecessor.

EXERCISE P5-2   The apostrophe   Before working this exercise, read section P5 in *A Writer's Reference,* Fifth Edition.

A. Each of the following sentences has two words containing apostrophes. Only one of the apostrophes is used correctly in each sentence. Delete or move the other apostrophe. Example:

Farther back in American history, one woman's soldiering had made her famous; no one has

                    hers.
yet had a story to match ~~her's.~~
                 ^

1. Deborah Sampson never dreamed that she would someday fight in battles' for American independence, much less that the battles' outcomes might depend on her.

2. Because her parents' income was not enough to support their children, Deborah was sent to live with relatives of her parents' in another town.

3. Later she was sent to live in a foster family with ten sons'; the sons' acceptance of her was wholehearted, and one son became her fiancé when she grew up.

4. The war was'nt over when news of his death reached Deborah; she wasn't long in making a major decision.

5. Using a false name, she enlisted to take his place — determined to mind her *p*'s and *q*s so well that she would not be detected.

B. The following sentences contain no apostrophes. Add any that are needed. If a sentence is correct, mark it "OK." Example:

Who's   *who's*
~~Whose~~ to say ~~whos~~ right about Deborah Sampson's decision?
^   ^

6. If men have the right to fight for their beliefs, should women have the right to fight for theirs?

7. Its clear that Deborah Sampson thought so; she enlisted twice to fight for hers.

8. On her first attempt, Sampson enlisted almost at the end of the day — and was discovered before its end arrived.

9. Though drinking was not a habit of hers, she spent her first evening as a soldier copying other new soldiers behavior.

10. Coming to the aid of this very noisy, very drunk, and very sick "buddy" of theirs, they soon were asking, "Whose this?"

EXERCISE P5-3   The apostrophe   Before working this exercise, read section P5 in *A Writer's Reference*, Fifth Edition.

Circle the correct form of the word in parentheses. The first one has been done for you.

Loreta Velazquez was not the only woman (who's, whose) help was used during the Civil War, nor was being a foot soldier the only way women served in that war.

She was not in combat, but Mary Walker, then in her (thirties, thirty's), served in the Union army. She served with such distinction that she became the first woman to receive the Medal of Honor, the (military's, militarys') highest-ranking medal. It is awarded only to members of the armed (forces, force's) and only for gallantry in action.

Mary (Walker's, Walkers) specialty was surgery. Just as shocking as her profession — the role of military surgeon was not (everyone's, everyones') idea of the proper role for a woman in the 1860s — were Dr. Walker's opinions on how women should dress. She said that women (shouldn't, should'nt) wear tight corsets because such corsets were injurious to (women's, womens') health. She even considered long skirts unhealthy. She felt so strongly on the subject of women's attire that she herself determined to wear long pants. Army (regulations, regulations') did not permit such attire for a woman. (Who's, Whose) permission was required for her to do so? It required special permission from the U.S. Congress, but Dr. Mary Walker finally won that battle of the Civil War.

She did not live to see the ending of her final battle. After the war, she went back to her private practice of medicine and began fighting for a constitutional amendment to allow women to vote. Congress passed the Twentieth Amendment in 1920. But Mary Walker died before (its, it's) adoption.

EXERCISE P5-4   The apostrophe: Guided review

In the following paragraph, add apostrophes where they are missing, and delete or correct them where they have been misused. Rule numbers in the margin refer to appropriate rules in section P5 of *A Writer's Reference,* Fifth Edition. The first revision has been done for you.

Deborah Sampson, who fought in America's Revolution, fulfilled her light infan-

tryman duties pretending to be a private named Robert Shurtlieff. To ~~anyones~~ *anyone's* ques-   *P5-b*

tions about where he was based, this private said, "West Point." Sampsons first enlist-   *P5-a*

ment lasted less than a day, but her second enlistment was different. It lasted until the

wars end, and along with many others she was honorably discharged from the Conti-   *P5-a*

nental Army on October 23, 1783. Throughout her service, it was everyones opinion that   *P5-b*

she was an excellent soldier. Her officers reports on her were always good. Wounded   *P5-a*

twice, she outwitted the doctors and returned to her unit undetected; but when she

came down with "the fevers," a doctor discovered the secret that until then had been

her's alone. (Many of the distinctions among different illnesses that produce fevers —   *P5-e*

from typhoid to influenza — were not yet known; if patients had a high fever and it's   *P5-e*

accompanying discomforts for very long, they were diagnosed as having "the fevers.")

Its no surprise that when her secret was finally told, her superior officers wouldnt be-   *P5-c, P5-c*

lieve it. Dressed in women's clothes, she was escorted to separate quarters not by the

M.P.s but by her superior officers. Many years later, at Paul Reveres' suggestion, she   *P5-a*

donned the uniform again and went on speaking tours' to raise much-needed money for   *P5-e*

her family and to secure a monthly pension from the army she had once served.

EXERCISE P6-1   Quotation marks: Guided practice

Edit the following sentences to correct the quotation marks and punctuation used with quotation marks. Rule numbers in the margin refer to appropriate rules in section P6 in *A Writer's Reference*, Fifth Edition. Answers to this exercise appear in the back of this book. Example:

> **The parents watched as the doctor bandaged the boy's eyes. "For the love of God, what can we do?" asked the father?.**
> P6-f

1. The doctor answered "You can do nothing but pray."   P6-f

2. When the bandages were removed and the shades were opened to let in the bright sunlight, the doctor asked, "What do you see"?   P6-f

3. "Nothing," said the boy. I see nothing.   P6-a

4. The village priest said "I have recently seen a remarkable school." He had just returned from a trip to Paris.   P6-f

5. "In this school, he added blind students are taught to read."   P6-a

6. "You didn't say "read," did you?" asked the boy's father.   P6-c

7. The boy responded to the priest's words as if they were a trick of some kind "Now you are joking with me. How can such a thing be possible?"   P6-f

8. The boy, Louis, thought it would be "great fun" to visit that school someday.   P6-g

9. His father promised "We will go soon, Louis."   P6-f

10. And so it happened that ten-year-old Louis Braille entered the National Institute for Blind Youths and began the long effort to erase the fear people had of even the word blind.   P6-e

EXERCISE P6-2   Quotation marks   Before working this exercise, read section P6 in *A Writer's Reference,* Fifth Edition.

Change each indirect quotation into a direct quotation, using correct punctuation and deleting or changing words as necessary. Example:

The doctor told them not to look for miracles.

The doctor said, "Do not look for miracles."

_____

1. The doctor added that in all probability their son would never see again.

    _____

    _____

2. Mr. Braille exclaimed that he had seen blind students at the institute making their own clothes and shoes.

    _____

    _____

3. The inventor of the military raised-dot system of writing told Louis to experiment all he wished but not to set his hopes too high.

    _____

    _____

4. When his old friends in the village saw him with his stylus and paper, they asked him if he was still punching away at it.

    _____

    _____

5. Louis asked the government official if he was blind and if he understood what it was like not to see.

    _____

    _____

EXERCISE P6-3   **Quotation marks**   Before working this exercise, read section P6 in *A Writer's Reference,* Fifth Edition.

In the following sentences, insert needed quotation marks and punctuation used with quotation marks. If a sentence is correct, mark it "OK." Example:

> **One of Braille's students wrote, "Attending his classes was a pleasure to enjoy rather than a duty to fulfill."**

1. Louis Braille asked the inventor of the military raised-dot system a serious question "Do you think it would be possible to change the symbols in some way, to reduce them in size?"

2. Barbier, the inventor of the system, replied "Of course. Anything is possible."

3. "I have hoped" said the founder of the institute "that this school would be a bright torch held aloft to bring light to the blind."

4. "I am going to instruct the teachers to begin using your system in the classroom," said the institute director. "You must understand, though, that your method has not yet been proved."

5. Louis Braille wanted a system so complete that people could read and write the words and music to a song like the Marseillaise, the French national anthem.

EXERCISE P6-4   Quotation marks: Guided review

Edit the following paragraphs to correct the use of quotation marks and punctuation used with quotation marks. Rule numbers in the margin refer to appropriate rules in section P6 of *A Writer's Reference,* Fifth Edition. The first revision has been made for you.

Louis Braille entered the National Institute for Blind Youths in Paris when he was ten. At twelve, he was already experimenting with a system of raised letters known as "night-~~writing~~" *writing,"* which was used by the military. Institute teachers decided that night- writing was impractical, but Louis became proficient at it. When Charles Barbier, inventor of the system, visited the institute, Louis told him "Your symbols are too large and too complicated. Impressed, Barbier encouraged him and said that "since Louis was blind himself, he might discover the magic key that had eluded his teachers."   *P6-f* / *P6-f* / *P6-a* / *P6-g*

Louis Braille wanted a system that would work for everything from a textbook on science to a poem like Heinrich Heine's Loreley. At fifteen, he had worked out his own system of six dots arranged in various patterns. "Read to me," he said to one of his teachers, and I will take down your words." As the teacher read, Louis punched his paper and then read the passage back without error. The teacher exclaimed, "Remarkable"! Government officials, not impressed enough to take any action, said simply that Braille should be encouraged. "You didn't say "encouraged," did you?" asked Braille. He wanted official acceptance, not simply encouragement. "The system has proved itself," said Louis. We have been using it for five years now."   *P6-d* / *P6-f* / *P6-f* / *P6-c* / *P6-f*

For most people, the word Braille itself now means simply a system of reading and writing used by blind people; for blind people, it means freedom and independence. Braille himself died before his system was recognized beyond the institute. The plaque on the house of his birth, however, records the world's recognition of his work with these words: He opened the doors of knowledge to all those who cannot see.   *P6-e* / *P6-a*

NOTE: For all the exercises in section P7, you will need to refer to the following poem.

The New Colossus

by Emma Lazarus

Not like the brazen giant of Greek fame,

With conquering limbs astride from land to land;

Here at our sea-washed, sunset gates shall stand

A mighty woman with a torch, whose flame

Is the imprisoned lightning, and her name

Mother of Exiles. From her beacon hand

Glows world-wide welcome; her mild eyes command

The air-bridged harbor that twin cities frame.

"Keep, ancient lands, your storied pomp!" cries she

With silent lips. "Give me your tired, your poor,

Your huddled masses yearning to breathe free,

The wretched refuse of your teeming shore,

Send these, the homeless, tempest-tost to me,

I lift my lamp beside the golden door."

EXERCISE P7-1   Other punctuation marks: Guided practice

Edit the following paragraphs for correct use of the period, question mark, exclamation point, dash, parentheses, brackets, ellipsis mark, and slash. Rule numbers in the margin refer to appropriate rules in section P7 of *A Writer's Reference,* Fifth Edition. The first revision has been done for you, and a suggested revision of these paragraphs appears in the back of this book.

The most famous woman in America is Miss Liberty‚a 450,000-pound, 154-foot   *P7-d*

resident of New York City. For people all over the world, the Statue of Liberty symbol-

izes America! Yet the idea for the statue did not come from America, England, or even   *P7-c*

New York itself. Where did the idea come from. It came from France. Three men can   *P7-b*

claim the credit for construction of Miss Liberty: Frédéric-Auguste Bartholdi, sculptor;

Alexandre-Gustave Eiffel, structural engineer; and Richard Morris Hunt, architect.

France gave the statue to the United States — and the United States provided the ped-   *P7-d*

estal on which it stands.

Two Americans contributed significantly to the statue. The first was Joseph Pulitzer,

then owner and publisher of the *New York World* (and a Russian immigrant). He led   *P7-e*

several fundraising efforts and urged every citizen to give what he/she could to help   *P7-h*

build the pedestal. The second American who contributed significantly was Emma

Lazarus. She wrote the famous lines on the bronze plaque inside the statue. Her three-

word title "The New Colossus" (huge statue) alludes to a statue built in the harbor of

Rhodes in ancient Greece. The most quoted lines from "The New Colossus" are probably

these: "Give me your tired, your poor, / Your huddled masses yearning to breathe free."

EXERCISE P7-2   **Other punctuation marks**   Before working this exercise, read section P7 in *A Writer's Reference,* Fifth Edition.

Edit the following sentences by using the punctuation indicated in brackets. Refer to the poem "The New Colossus" as necessary. Example:

Bartholdi's Statue of Liberty‾‾better known in France as *Liberty Enlightening the* World‾‾celebrated ideals that France and America shared. [*Dashes*]

1. America's Revolution celebrated liberty. The French added two more words to form the battle cry of the French Revolution, "Liberty, Equality, and Fraternity." [*Dash*]

2. Emma Lazarus understood Bartholdi's desire to demonstrate this common interest. In the eight words of her opening line, "Not like the brazen giant of Greek fame (the Colossus of Rhodes)," she alludes to an ancient statue one hundred feet high. [*Brackets*]

3. Bartholdi was determined to build "A mighty woman — Mother of Exiles" and place her in New York Harbor. [*Ellipsis mark*]

4. He traveled all over America, to Boston, Chicago, Denver, Salt Lake City, and many other places, to promote his idea. [*Dashes*]

5. He was amazed at the country's size, industry, and enthusiasm for creating things, buildings, that is, not art. [*Parentheses*]

6. Bartholdi discovered that money, the enthusiasm of U.S. citizens, and political support, all necessary for his project, were hard to get. [*Parentheses*]

7. He decided on a novel, hands-on approach, allowing people to climb into completed parts of the statue. [*Dash*]

8. Three cities were chosen: [1] In Philadelphia, the hand and torch attracted Centennial Exhibition visitors; [2] in New York, the same exhibit drew people downtown; and [3] in Paris, visitors explored the head and shoulders. [*Parentheses*]

9. When more money was needed, wealthy newspaper publisher Joseph Pulitzer, an immigrant himself, turned to nonwealthy Americans, working-class men, women, and children, and it was their small gifts that paid for the statue's pedestal. [*Dashes*]

10. Their gifts allowed Miss Liberty's torch to shine out over the water to say, "Send these, the homeless, tempest-tost to me, I lift my lamp beside the golden door." [*Slash*]

EXERCISE P7-3   Other punctuation marks   Before working this exercise, read
section P7 in *A Writer's Reference,* Fifth Edition.

The dashes, parentheses, brackets, ellipsis marks, and slashes in the following sentences are not
well used. Edit the sentences to be more effective by deleting punctuation marks, replacing them
with other marks, or restructuring the sentences. Refer to "The New Colossus" as necessary. Example:

**On October 29, 1886 ⧸, one hundred and ten years after the Declaration of Independence, ⧸
Miss Liberty was formally dedicated.**

1. Miss Liberty was the only woman at her dedication (except for two Frenchwomen who came
   with the sculptor).

2. On that day, the Lady who was such a contrast to the "brazen giant of Greek fame" [the Colossus of Rhodes] was almost obscured from view by rain and wind.

3. Also, the crowds of people pushing and shoving resembled the ". . . huddled masses" Emma
   Lazarus wrote about.

4. The crowd — crushed together — trying to listen to the main speaker — he was William M.
   Evarts — could hear other voices too.

5. Women who were angry about being excluded from the ceremony had sailed in close to the
   island (they had chartered a boat) and were yelling their protests.

6. With all of the noise from the crowd and/or the women, the speaker paused.

7. He paused so long that an aide thought the speech was over. The aide signaled Bartholdi (who
   had been waiting inside the statue).

8. Bartholdi saw the signal and unveiled the statue . . . an hour early.

9. The plaque with Emma Lazarus's poem on it was not on the statue at this time; it was added
   later — in 1903 — without any special attention.

10. It is still there today for all visitors to read/ponder as they meet America's most beloved lady.

EXERCISE P7-4   Other punctuation marks: Guided review

Edit the following paragraphs for most effective use of the period, question mark, exclamation point, dash, parentheses, bracket, ellipsis mark, and slash. Refer to "The New Colossus" as necessary. Rule numbers in the margin refer to appropriate rules in section P7 of *A Writer's Reference,* Fifth Edition. The first revision has been done for you.

           fourteen-line
The sonnet is a poem ——of fourteen lines—— with a particular pattern to its rhymes;   *P7-d*

it is often used to compare or contrast two items. Emma Lazarus's poem "The New

Colossus" is a sonnet. Lazarus uses its fourteen lines to contrast two statues. One, the

ancient Colossus of Rhodes (which was male) represented the sun god; the other, the   *P7-e*

new Colossus, was female and represented Liberty. The Rhodes Colossus symbolized

what Lazarus calls "storied pomp." The French-made American one stood for freedom

and opportunity.

In her first line, "Not like the brazen (bronze) giant of Greek fame," Lazarus refers   *P7-f*

to the material of which the old Colossus was made. Bronze, a valuable metal when the

Colossus of Rhodes was erected in 280 B.C., was available only to the wealthy. Miss

Liberty was made of copper, a material available to all classes of people! When Miss   *P7-c*

Liberty was erected in 1898, America's least valuable coin, the one-cent piece, was made

from copper. Miss Liberty was for everyone, not just the wealthy.

The major contrast Lazarus sets up is in the attitudes of the two statues. What is

the difference in attitude conveyed by the two statues. The old Colossus is powerful, not   *P7-b*

caring about the "wretched refuse" of its "teeming shore." The new one welcomes them

all: "Send these, the homeless, tempest-tost to me, I lift my lamp beside the golden   *P7-h*

door."

Unit review: Editing for punctuation (P1–P7)

Edit the following paragraphs to correct errors in punctuation or to use more effective punctuation. Rule numbers in the margin refer to appropriate rules in sections P1–P7 of *A Writer's Reference,* Fifth Edition. The first revision has been done for you.

The outside of the Statue of Liberty is made of copper**,** but what is inside the   *P1-a*
statue. Inside the statue are: iron braces and staircases. The thin copper plates that   *P7-b, P4-d*
form the outside of the statue are bolted to a network of iron braces. There are several
staircases allowing workers and tourists to climb all the way into the head and the
torch. (This intricate network of braces and stairways was designed by Alexandre-
Gustave Eiffel; the same man who designed the famous Eiffel Tower in Paris.)   *P3-d*

For some years, the lighting equipment for Miss Libertys torch was also inside.   *P5-a*
Soon after the statue was set up for example engineers tried Edison's new invention,   *P1-f*
the electric lightbulb. They cut holes in the torch's copper sheets and hung lightbulbs
inside. Later the copper sheets came down and glass windows went up. Giving Miss
Liberty a light that everyone would recognize as hers, challenged engineers and design-   *P2-b*
ers for sixty more years. When the statue was restored in the 1980s part of the lighting   *P1-b*
equipment went outside. Floodlights were installed on the torch's balcony, and focused   *P2-a*
on thin gold sheets that form the torch "... whose flame / Is the imprisoned lightning.   *P7-g, P6-a*
Miss Liberty will be able to welcome newcomers for many years.

EXERCISE M1/M2/M3-1   Spelling, the hyphen, and capitalization: Guided practice

Correct any errors in spelling and in the use of the hyphen and capital letters in the following paragraphs. Rule numbers in the margin refer to appropriate rules in sections M1, M2, and M3 of *A Writer's Reference,* Fifth Edition. The first revision has been done for you, and a revision of these paragraphs appears in the back of this book.

Everyone has heard of Christopher Columbus, but not many people know much about him. Most people remember that he discovered America in A.D. 1492. Some people know that he had three ships, but they might not be sure ~~weather~~ *whether* they could name   *M1-b* them. (The ships were the *Niña,* the *Pinta,* and the *Santa María.*) A few people might even remember that Columbus thought he had found the Indies. And those with great self confidence might be willing to guess at the number of trips he made to his India. (It   *M2-d* was four.) Probably no one would be familiar with his favorite word, *adelante.*

If they were asked what Columbus was trying to prove with his expensive journey, most people would reply that he was trying to prove the world was round. They would be wrong. If they were asked what Columbus meant by "the indies," they would prob-   *M3-a* ably say "India." They would be wrong again. If they were asked what Columbus's rank was, they would most likely say "Captain." They would be wrong again. If they were   *M3-a* asked what his sailors feared most, a number of them would reply, "they feared that the   *M3-e* boats would fall off the edge of the earth." And they would be wrong again.

Isn't it strange that people can be so ignorant about a well known man like Colum-   *M2-b* bus?

EXERCISE M1/M2/M3-2   **Spelling**   Before working this exercise, read sections M1, M2, and M3 in *A Writer's Reference,* Fifth Edition.

Edit the following sentences to correct spelling errors. (Hint: There are ten errors.) Example:

>   *incredibly*   *believed*
> **Others may have considered him ~~incredibally~~ lucky, but Columbus ~~beleived~~ he had been called**
> **by God to be the one to find a new way to the Indies.**

1. To begin with, he was born in Genoa, Italy, the best place concievable for someone who wanted to be in the sailing busness, since Genoa was a major seaport.

2. Other people said his being born there was all "just chance"; Columbus prefered to think that it was part of God's arrangment for him.

3. He was not suprised to be the sole survivor of a shipwreck that occured when he was twenty-five.

4. Weather others excepted the idea or not, Columbus knew he survived such a disasterous event because God had plans for him.

5. He thought that even his name emphasized his calling: *Christopher* means "Christ-bearing," and he would take Christ's name to the heatherns in India.

EXERCISE M1/M2/M3-3   **The hyphen**   If you have problems with this exercise, see section M2 in *A Writer's Reference,* Fifth Edition.

The writer of the following sentences got hyphen-happy. Remove seven of the twelve hyphens. If a sentence needs no hyphens removed, mark it "OK." Example:

> **Columbus's all-consuming goal made him think that God͟himself had worked͟out the fortu-**
> **itous marriage Columbus made in 1478.**

1. Marrying into a noble-family when he was thirty-three gave Columbus direct-access to the king of Portugal.

2. When the king firmly-declined Columbus's request to finance an exploratory-voyage, this well-known sailor decided he was supposed to go to Spain.

3. Queen Isabella was anxious to make everyone into a practicing-Christian; because Columbus was religious, she did not consider the voyage a half-witted proposal.

4. After his discovery of "India," Columbus received confirmation of his self-given title, Admiral of the Ocean Seas and Viceroy of the Indies.

5. When the *Santa María* was wrecked, Columbus saw the incident as his God-given opportunity to go back post-haste to Spain, get more men, and return to this newly-found land.

EXERCISE M1/M2/M3-4   Capitalization   Before working this exercise, read sections M1, M2, and M3 in *A Writer's Reference,* Fifth Edition.

Edit the following paragraphs to correct errors in capitalization. The first sentence has been edited for you.

If Columbus had made his return trip first, he might not have been so eager to set out for the
Indies
~~indies~~. The voyage turned out all right, but it had its bad times.

To begin with, the *Niña* and the *Pinta* were separated on the way back to Spain. The weather was very bad, especially when the two ships ran into a storm west of the Azores. The *Niña* almost sank. Columbus was so sure it was going down that he put a record of his Discoveries in a small barrel, sealed it completely, and threw it overboard. That way, if the ship went down, there was still a chance that someone would learn of his discoveries. Actually, the ship made it to Santa María, a portuguese island. The authorities there thought Columbus was lying about his adventures and arrested the crew. The crew was released only because Columbus threatened to shoot up the town.

The *Niña* was thrown off course again, but then Columbus's luck turned. The boat came into Lisbon, and Columbus was a guest of king John II for a brief time before he took off for Spain again. Finally, the *Niña* made it home. On March 15, 1493, it sailed into the Harbor at Palos. The *Pinta* arrived shortly afterward on the same day. Such a coincidence certainly seemed to be a sign of divine approval and delighted Columbus. When queen Isabella saw what Columbus had brought back, she was impressed. She thought that god had surely had a hand in the matter. Certainly many influences had played a part in his success that Spring. Even Marco Polo's book *Description of the world* had played a role: Getting Columbus started on the journey. Columbus was convinced that his life was just one miracle after another. "i've been chosen," he might have said. "God has chosen me."

EXERCISE M1/M2/M3-5   Spelling, the hyphen, and capitalization: Guided review

Edit the following paragraphs to correct misspellings and errors in the use of the hyphen and capital letters. Rule numbers in the margin refer to appropriate rules in sections M1, M2, and M3 of *A Writer's Reference,* Fifth Edition. The first revision has been done for you.

As difficult as Columbus's return to Spain from his first exploration was, the reception at court quite made up for it. Columbus certainly made an all-out effort to *M2-d* impress the court, the city, and the entire country. Lavishly attired, he received a grand welcome as he led his entourage into Barcelona, the Spanish capital. It must have been a sight to behold: A procession like none Barcelona had ever seen before. Leading the *M3-f* parade was a gaudily bedecked horse carrying Columbus, followed by six captive "indians" and all the crew. Everyone but Columbus was carrying boxes, baskets, and *M3-a* cages full of interesting and exotic items.

When the group reached the throne room, King Ferdinand and Queen Isabella stood up to greet Columbus formally and to admire his apron covered captives. Colum- *M2-b* bus asked the royal couple to except gifts of plants, shells, darts, thread, and gold. As *M1-b* intrigued as they were with the other gifts, King Ferdinand and Queen Isabella basically wanted gold. Luckily, Columbus had collected enough samples of it to satisfy them.

By the end of the first week home, Columbus had such prestige that everyone wanted to accommodate the wishes of the Italian sailor at the court of Spain. Columbus had no doubt that he would receive a Commission for a second voyage of exploration or *M3-a* even colonization.

EXERCISE M4/M5/M6-1   Abbreviations, numbers, and italics: Guided practice

Correct any errors in the use of abbreviations, numbers, and italics (underlining) in the following paragraphs. Rule numbers in the margin refer to appropriate rules in sections M4, M5, and M6 of *A Writer's Reference,* Fifth Edition. The first revision has been done for you, and a revision of these paragraphs appears in the back of this book.

After being feted, feasted, and honored on his return from his first voyage across the ocean, Columbus must have told and retold the story of his trip. He would have told listeners how, after the ships had sailed for ~~3~~ *three* weeks, his men threatened to turn back   *M5-a*
because they had never sailed so far west before. Columbus, sure of his special calling as an explorer, *promised* them that they would sight land within three days. On the   *M6-e*
evening of the third day, at ten o'clock, he thought he saw a light and alerted a nearby servant. Both of them lost sight of it almost at once. But at two o'clock the next a.m., a   *M4-c*
cannon shot sounded from the Pinta. "Land! Land!" cried the sailors. Columbus had   *M6-b*
kept his promise.

Retelling the story of his voyage, Columbus would have described the beautiful island that the ships first landed on. He named it San Salvador. He would have told how, at every island he and his men visited, natives had flocked to the boats to see the strangers; e.g., one day, more than a thousand people had come in just one hour. Colum-   *M4-d*
bus spent three months exploring and setting up a fort before leaving for the return trip to Spain. And on their return, 8 months later, he and his crew received a royal welcome.   *M5-a*

Yes, he had had a few problems on the trip out, and the return trip had been very hard, but the memories of that first voyage were indelibly imprinted on Columbus's brain.

EXERCISE M4/M5/M6-2   Abbreviations and numbers   Before working this exercise, read sections M4, M5, and M6 in *A Writer's Reference,* Fifth Edition.

A. Edit the following sentences to correct errors in the use of abbreviations. Mark the one correct sentence "OK." Example:

> **The sailors who went with Columbus had the same four directions sailors still use:**
> *north, south, east, and west.*
> ~~N, S, E, and W.~~
> ^

1. Sailors in A.D. 1492 knew the world was round; they were not afraid of sailing off the edge of the world.

2. They worried about more serious things, e.g., whether the wind would blow both ways so they could get back home to Spain.

3. They also weren't sure about distances; however, one famous Italian prof., Dr. Toscanelli, thought he knew.

4. He was willing to estimate the distance from Lisbon, Port., to Japan.

5. He said that the exact no. of miles between the two places was three thousand nautical miles.

B. Edit the following sentences to correct errors in the use of numbers. Mark the one correct sentence "OK." Example:

>   *three*
> **Dr. Toscanelli set the distance at ~~3~~ thousand nautical miles.**
>   ^

6. In twelve ninety-eight, Marco Polo had written a book about his travels to the Indies.

7. 7,448 islands were in the Indies, according to Marco Polo's book, as well as India, China, the East Indies, and Japan.

8. Columbus was 41 when he convinced Queen Isabella to send him to find those islands.

9. As part of the contract, Columbus demanded ten % of the treasure he brought back to Spain.

10. At 8:00 A.M. on August 3, 1492, Columbus set out from Spain for the Indies.

EXERCISE M4/M5/M6-3 **Italics (underlining)** Before working this exercise, read sections M4, M5, and M6 in *A Writer's Reference,* Fifth Edition.

Edit the following sentences to correct the use of italics (underlining). Example:

Marco Polo's book was named <u>Description of the World</u>.

1. On the "Niña," the "Pinta," and the "Santa María" Columbus had one hundred men, all kinds of supplies, and enough cats to control the rat population.

2. Columbus always spoke the same word to his men — Adelante! (That means "Forward!" or "Sail on!")

3. Marco Polo's book Description of the World had not prepared the men for seeing the same horizon week after week.

4. To every fear or complaint, Columbus simply replied "Forward!" and that word forward began to get on the sailors' nerves.

5. Columbus offered a special reward — a silk jacket — to the first man who spotted *land.*

EXERCISE M4/M5/M6-4   Abbreviations, numbers, and italics: Guided review

Correct any errors in the use of abbreviations, numbers, and italics in the following paragraphs. Rule numbers in the margin refer to appropriate rules in sections M4, M5, and M6 of *A Writer's Reference,* Fifth Edition. The first revision has been done for you.

Columbus's first voyage, in 1492 ~~A.D.~~ *A.D.* had been successful. Pleased with the gifts   *M4-c*

he had brought and impressed by his reports, King Ferdinand and Queen Isabella quickly

ordered him to organize another voyage. Columbus was delighted to do so. At first his

luck held. Led by the flagship Maríagalante, a fleet of 17 ships and a thousand men who   *M6-b, M5-a*

wanted to colonize the new land made the second trip in twenty-one days. Columbus's

good fortune, however, did not last. Life went downhill for the Italian sailor from that

time on.

The so-called Admiral of the Ocean Sea (a title Columbus had given himself) had

one disastrous experience after another. When he got back to the recently settled new

town he had left, the whole settlement had been destroyed, and the 39 men he had left   *M5-a*

there were all dead. Columbus quickly found a new spot for his new colony, the first

European colony in America. The new site had two drawbacks: bad water and many

mosquitoes. Embarrassed, Columbus had to send Queen Isabella's ships back for help;

he loaded them not with gold but with pepper, sandalwood, and a no. of exotic birds.   *M4-c*

Other voyages followed, but each turned out worse than the one before it. Not even

his favorite word, *adelante,* seemed to work for Columbus anymore. His 1st voyage had   *M4-e*

definitely been the most successful.

Unit review: Mechanics (M1–M6)

This essay has eleven errors in spelling and mechanics. Rule numbers in the margin refer to appropriate rules in sections M1–M6 of *A Writer's Reference,* Fifth Edition. The first revision has been done for you. Correct the ten other errors.

Columbus made an all-out effort to find the Indies — India, China, the East *M2-d*
Indies, and Japan. Instead, he found Cuba, Venezuela, the Bahamas, and the coasts of
South and Central America. Unable to find gold, he captured 5 hundred natives and *M5-a*
had them shipped back to Spain to be sold as slaves. He punished the natives so se-
verely when they did not bring him gold that in two years one third of them ran away or *M2-c*
were killed or sold. Things went from bad to worse; e.g., many settlers died of illness, *M4-d*
and some went back to Spain with bad reports of his governance. Convinced that God
was unhappy with him for some transgression, Columbus returned to Spain wearing a
monk's course garb and walking humbly. People gave him a new title, Columbus, *M1-b*
admiral of the Mosquitoes. *M3-b*

Ferdinand and Isabella gave him another opportunity, though, and on May
thirtieth, 1498, Columbus set out again. The voyage was a disaster, with Columbus *M5-b*
ending up back in Spain, this time in chains. Columbus got one more chance, but hurri-
canes and storms plagued him. He wrote, "other tempests have I seen, but none so long *M3-e*
or so grim as this." He must by now have realized that Dr. Toscanelli did not no his *M1-b*
geography very well. Yet "Sail on!" was still his answer to *every* setback. *M6-e*

When he got back to Spain, sick and exhausted, queen Isabella died before he *M3-b*
could see her. Columbus died still insisting he had found the Indies. He had not, of
course. He had done far more: He had discovered a new world.

EXERCISE B1-1   Parts of speech: Preview   Before working this exercise, read
section B1 in *A Writer's Reference,* Fifth Edition.

In the following paragraphs, label the part of speech of each italicized word. Use these codes: noun (N), pronoun (PN), helping verb (HV), main verb (MV), adjective (ADJ), adverb (ADV), preposition (P), conjunction (C). The first word has been marked for you, and answers to this exercise appear in the back of this book.

America's Declaration of Independence *seems* very formal to today's *readers.* Many of its sentences *are* long and involved, and some *of* its words seem old fashioned. But *its* central message is loud *and* clear to all those who take the time to read and understand it, whether they are schoolchildren *or* adult immigrants.

Those somewhat *formal* words contain both a declaration and a promise. The Declaration *starts* with a seventy-one word statement called the "Preamble." It *simply* says that when one group of people break their ties *with* another, those people *should* tell *everyone* their reasons for breaking up.

In the next part, called the "Declaration of Rights," the colonists list their basic assumptions *about* life — that everyone is born with *certain* rights ("life, liberty, and the pursuit of happiness"), that governments have power only *when* people give it to *them,* and that when a government repeatedly *acts* in ways that deny people's rights, people have a right and a duty to overthrow that *government* and build another one.

It was a *bold* beginning for a bold document — a declaration promising freedom that has *been* celebrated by Americans for more than two hundred years.

EXERCISE B1-2   Nouns and noun/adjectives   Before working this exercise, read section B1-a in *A Writer's Reference,* Fifth Edition.

A. Each of the following word groups contains only one noun. Circle the noun. Example:

national   nationwide   (nation)

1. defendable   defend   defenses
2. speaking   speaker   speak
3. just   justice   justly
4. normal   normally   normality
5. repetition   repeating   repeated

B. Underline the nouns (and noun/adjectives) in the following sentences. There are four in each sentence. Example:

> When they apply for American citizenship, refugee immigrants must study some famous American documents.

6. Schoolchildren and new citizens have similar homework assignments.
7. They both must learn the pledge of allegiance to the country's flag.
8. Many of these people also memorize the opening words of the Declaration of Independence.
9. The Preamble to the Constitution is often assigned, as well as some famous speeches and the national anthem.
10. If students pass their tests on all this, they are promoted; if immigrants pass theirs, they are welcomed into American citizenship.

EXERCISE B1-3 **Pronouns and pronoun/adjectives** Before working this exercise, read section B1-b in *A Writer's Reference,* Fifth Edition.

A. Circle the five pronouns in each group of words. Example:

(his)   (they)   under   (whoever)   (no one)   (themselves)

1. I	she	of	he	ours	everyone
2. her	me	it	to	whose	many
3. for	him	you	us	this	someone
4. they	my	that	we	from	some
5. in	them	mine	your	these	nothing
6. at	yours	her	his	all	none
7. hers	our	its	nobody	another	over
8. under	myself	their	yours	each	several
9. from	theirs	who	which	either	something
10. whom	those	any	both	few	through

B. Underline the pronouns (including pronoun/adjectives) in the following sentences. Except in the example, there are two in each sentence. Example:

<u>Our</u> Declaration of Independence includes <u>these</u> famous words: "<u>We</u> hold <u>these</u> truths to be self-evident."

11. Whoever reads the Declaration of Independence finds a message for everyone.

12. It says that all people are created equal.

13. Furthermore, the Declaration declares, "They are endowed by their creator with certain un-alienable rights."

14. "Among these rights are life, liberty, and the pursuit of happiness" may be its most famous line.

15. Refugees who apply for citizenship are claiming those rights.

EXERCISE B1-4 **Verbs** Before working this exercise, read section B1-c in *A Writer's Reference*, Fifth Edition.

A. All of the following paired sentences contain some form of the word *promise*. In each pair, circle the letter of the sentence that uses a form of the word *promise* as a verb. (Hint: The words *promised* and *promising* can sometimes function as adjectives.)

    a. The founders of this country made certain promises to each other.

    b. Each document of this country promises special things to the people who live here.

1a. In a way, the Constitution is a set of promises.

  b. The government promises to do certain things for citizens.

2a. In turn, the citizens must promise to obey certain laws.

  b. The citizens' promise is just as important as the government's.

3a. Some early citizens thought the Constitution had not promised them enough rights.

  b. They thought that the promised rights were not specific enough.

4a. By adding a Bill of Rights to the Constitution, citizens demanded a promise about freedom of religion.

  b. The Bill of Rights does indeed promise freedom of religion.

5a. One of the most promising signs of political health in the colonies was their insistence on gaining certain rights.

  b. Whenever citizens repeat their oath of allegiance, they are promising anew to honor the Constitution.

B. Underline all verbs in the paragraph below and label them "MV" (main verb) or "HV" (helping verb) above the line. The first sentence has been done for you.

        HV   MV

Who should vote? All citizens should go to the polls and vote. When citizens do this, they are making important choices that can affect their lives and the lives of others. In addition, citizens must tell their elected representatives how they feel about certain issues. If the representatives ignore these messages, they may lose their jobs. It is important that these representatives stay in touch with the voters, but it is just as important that the voters send messages. Without this kind of communication, America's great democratic experiment will fail.

EXERCISE B1-5   Adjectives and adverbs   Before working this exercise, read sections B1-d and B1-e in *A Writer's Reference,* Fifth Edition.

A. Label each of the following words as an adjective (ADJ) or an adverb (ADV). You should find twelve adjectives and eight adverbs. Example:

clean _ADJ_

1. inexpensive _____
2. very _____
3. rude _____
4. not _____
5. crazy _____
6. lovely _____
7. extremely _____

8. beautiful _____
9. sometimes _____
10. political _____
11. ten _____
12. never _____
13. tired _____
14. aloud _____

15. rich _____
16. lonely _____
17. oily _____
18. slowly _____
19. always _____
20. common _____

B. Label the adjectives (ADJ) and adverbs (ADV) in the following sentences. Ignore the articles *a, an,* and *the.* You should find ten adjectives and five adverbs. Example:

                                                      ADJ   ADV   ADJ

The Constitution and the Bill of Rights are separate, but they go together as a single document.

21. The Bill of Rights is the ten amendments that immediately follow the Constitution.

22. The First Amendment is the most familiar of the famous rights.

23. It guarantees religious freedom and freedom of speech for American citizens.

24. It also guarantees freedom of the press, an extremely important freedom in a democratic country.

25. Because representatives to the original Congress valued the right to discuss legislation publicly, the Bill of Rights assures citizens of the right to hold meetings and to petition the federal government.

EXERCISE B1-6   Prepositions   Before working this exercise, read section B1-f in *A Writer's Reference,* Fifth Edition.

A. Many prepositions express opposite ideas. Fill in the blanks below with prepositions that express the opposite idea to the one listed. Examples:

like ___*unlike*___   **into** ___*out of*___

1. above _____   6. after _____

2. against _____   7. down _____

3. in _____   8. inside _____

4. on _____   9. over _____

5. to _____   10. with _____

B. Circle all twenty prepositions in the following paragraph.

The men who wrote the Declaration of Independence dealt with many political controversies. In addition, they disagreed about many ideas. During their discussions, some still felt they should come to terms with England, some insisted on giving all of the reasons for their break with England, and some were against war under the existing circumstances. They argued over these issues frequently, making agreement seem impossible at first. They stuck to their task despite many disagreements between individuals, and in the end they put their feelings into words that remain famous today.

EXERCISE B1-7 Prepositions and conjunctions Before working this exercise, read sections B1-f and B1-g in *A Writer's Reference,* Fifth Edition.

In the following sentences, label all prepositions (P), coordinating conjunctions (CC), and subordinating conjunctions (SUB). The numbers in the brackets after each sentence indicate how many of each you should find. Example:

> *SUB*   *P*   *P*   *CC*
> **When the Bill of Rights was adopted, it gave to American citizens rights and guarantees none**
> *P*   *CC*
> **of the colonists or their predecessors had enjoyed. [3P, 2CC, 1SUB]**

1. When the founders of the United States wrote the Bill of Rights, they were recalling their past troubles with England. [3P, 1SUB]

2. They were also hoping that this new country and its laws would be different. [1CC, 1SUB]

3. Before the American Revolution, English officers and their men had been quartered in colonists' homes. [2P, 1CC]

4. The colonists often objected, but they could do nothing about the situation. [1P, 1CC]

5. Although they petitioned and appealed, nothing changed. [1CC, 1SUB]

6. Because the colonists objected to this practice, they put a special amendment about it in the Bill of Rights. [4P, 1SUB]

7. The amendment says that the government cannot make people give free room and board to soldiers unless the country is at war. [2P, 1CC, 2SUB]

8. Another problem was that, although the colonists objected, under English rule they and their homes could be searched by any magistrate or his appointees. [2P, 2CC, 2SUB]

9. Another amendment to the Bill of Rights would protect citizens from unreasonable searches; searching a citizen's home would require a warrant. [3P]

10. Because the Bill of Rights was added to the Constitution, Americans are still protected from these and several other intrusions by the government. [4P, 1CC, 1SUB]

EXERCISE B1-8   Parts of speech: Review   Before working this exercise, read section B1 in *A Writer's Reference,* Fifth Edition.

_____

In the following paragraphs, label the parts of speech of the italicized words. Use these codes: noun (N), pronoun (PN), helping verb (HV), main verb (MV), adjective (ADJ), adverb (ADV), preposition (P), and conjunction (C). The first word has been marked for you.

                               ADJ
    Americans fought a long *hard* war to secure the freedoms and rights that *their* Declaration had proclaimed. Even *while* the war was going on, France (America's ally) *was* trying to get America to agree *to* a truce. France proposed a treaty that *would* give America its independence *without* any questions. But under the French *proposal,* the boundaries of America would be established *by* which country's army was *currently* in control of the land. That would give Spain *and* France control of major portions *of* the land Americans claimed. John Adams, America's *negotiator,* refused to discuss such a plan.

    Adams was simply carrying out the spirit of the Declaration that had started the war. In the final *section* of their Declaration of Independence, the Americans had *used* another impossibly long sentence — more than one hundred words — to declare their separation from Great Britain and their determination to make their own decisions. They could *not* then have known how *costly* defending that Declaration would be. *But* when the war was over, the colonists had won the rights for which *they* had pledged to each other their lives, their fortunes, and their *sacred* honor.

EXERCISE B2-1   Parts of sentences: Preview   Before working this exercise, read section B2 in *A Writer's Reference,* Fifth Edition.

Label the function of each italicized word or word group in the following paragraphs. Use these abbreviations: subject (S), verb (V), subject complement (SC), direct object (DO), indirect object (IO), and object complement (OC). The first sentence has been done for you, and answers to this exercise appear in the back of this book.

               S   V   DO

New art *forms* often *lead* the *public* to a new way of looking at things. Frequently, however, viewers are not yet ready to understand the new forms.

A *group* of French artists *had* this *problem* in the 1800s. These artists completely changed their way of painting. Instead of painting in the subdued, dark tones of a formal studio, *they* often *went* outdoors. One of their new techniques was the use of color. *They* nearly always *gave* their *paintings* great *bursts* of color like sunlight on a field. Art *lovers* in France *were surprised* by such bright colors on the artists' canvases. People often called such paintings "open-air paintings." These *artists* usually *made* even their indoor *scenes* very *bright* with light and colors. Through an open window onto a bouquet of flowers or a bright-haired child *would pour* bright *sunshine*. *Were* Pierre-Auguste Renoir's *paintings* always *bright* and *cheerful*? Yes, and those of Claude Monet, Camille Pissarro, and Paul Cézanne were equally pleasant. These *painters,* now called "impressionists," *are admired* all over the world today, but in their own time the artists had to educate their viewers.

Twentieth-century artists had the same problem. Two new art *forms* from that period *are* good *examples,* "op art" and "pop art." *Both* of these *showed* their *viewers* everyday *objects* in quite different ways. Both eventually attracted a following. But like many artists before them, the op-art and pop-art painters had to educate their viewers.

EXERCISE B2-2   Subjects   Before working this exercise, read section B2-a in *A Writer's Reference*, Fifth Edition.

A. Each of the following sentences has three words or word groups italicized. One of these words or word groups is the subject. Find it and label it "S." Example:

S
Many *artists* have *preferred* certain colors for their *work*.

1. During one *part* of his life, *Picasso* preferred the color *blue*.

2. *There* are many famous *paintings* from *this* period.

3. *"Blue"* refers not only to the predominant *color* of these paintings but also to their *mood*.

4. In these paintings *you* will find *outcasts* or victims of *society* as the main characters.

5. Do the *derelicts and beggars* in these pictures reflect *Picasso's* own sense of *isolation*?

B. In the following paragraph, complete subjects have been italicized. Label the simple subject (or subjects) "SS." The first sentence has been done for you.

SS   SS
Pierre-Auguste Renoir and his young friends founded a new movement called "impressionism." Instead of trying to reproduce a scene exactly, *impressionist painters like Renoir and his friends* blended small brush strokes of different colors to give a general impression of a scene. Up close, *a careful observer of a restaurant scene* sees no solid edges on a table or a lady's hat, just small dabs of paint. At a distance, however, *that same careful observer* will see clearly the picture in the artist's mind. At first *the art world* laughed at and rejected the new movement. However, there is now *no serious argument about the importance of the impressionist movement*.

EXERCISE B2-3   **Direct objects and subject complements**   Before working this
exercise, read section B2-b in *A Writer's Reference,* Fifth Edition.

A. Subjects and verbs have been labeled in the following sentences. Label the italicized word as a
   simple direct object (DO) or a simple subject complement (SC). Example:

   s   v   *SC*
   Pierre-Auguste Renoir's parents were *supportive* of their son's ambitions.

   1. Renoir's love of art was *clear* to his parents.
   2. When he was a *boy* of thirteen, they apprenticed *him* to a porcelain artist.
   3. Renoir first learned the potter's *trade.*
   4. Soon he was quite *skillful* at making and firing vases.
   5. He enjoyed the *task* of decorating the vases even more.

B. Using the pattern of each sentence as a model, write a short sentence of your own on any subject.
   Example:

   S/V/SC: Renoir was an artist.

   Casey was a ballplayer.
   _____

   6. S/V: Renoir studied.

   _____

   7. S/V: Renoir studied hard.

   _____

   8. S/V/SC: He became an excellent painter.

   _____

   9. S/V/SC: His paintings are cheerful.

   _____

   10. S/V/DO: Café owners liked his murals.

   _____

EXERCISE B2-4   Indirect objects and object complements   Before working this exercise, read section B2-b in *A Writer's Reference,* Fifth Edition.

A. Subjects, verbs, and direct objects are labeled in the following sentences. Label the italicized word as a simple indirect object (IO) or a simple object complement (OC). Example:

                S   V   *IO*   DO
Renoir's parents gave *him* a good start in his chosen profession.

                                    S   V   DO
1. Besides his parents, other people considered the young Renoir a fine *painter*.

      S   V   DO
2. He had shown local *businessmen* some of his work.

        S   V   DO
3. Owners of some Paris cafés gave *him* painting jobs.

       S   V   DO
4. He made the walls of their cafés *beautiful*.

                   S   V   DO
5. The lovely scenes made both customers and owners *happy*.

B. Using the pattern of each sentence as a model, write a short sentence of your own on any subject. Example:

    S/V/DO/OC: Renoir called his style of painting "impressionist."

             Casey called his style of batting "the best." _____

6. S/V/IO/DO: Paris café owners offered Renoir much work.

_____

7. S/V/IO/DO: They gave him twenty orders for murals.

_____

8. S/V/DO/OC: They considered his work exceptional.

_____

9. S/V/DO/OC: People called him "the happy painter."

_____

10. S/V: His popularity increased.

_____

EXERCISE B2-5   Direct objects, indirect objects, and object complements
Before working this exercise, read section B2-b in *A Writer's Reference,* Fifth Edition.

Underline the verb of each sentence. Then label the complete direct object (DO) and any complete indirect objects (IO) or object complements (OC). Example:

┌─*DO*─┐   ┌────*DO*────┐┌────*OC*────┐
Many people <u>enjoy</u> pop art. They <u>find</u> this new kind of art a refreshing change.

1. During World War II, American mass media flooded London.

2. The effect of that flood fascinated many London artists.

3. Using the American material, British artists gave the world a new art form.

4. To produce their art, the artists used images from popular culture.

5. Someone named the new art "pop art."

6. Most Americans find pop art very appealing.

7. To some, it reflects the optimism of the 1960s.

8. Items like flags, signs, and comic strips gave pop artists their subject matter.

9. Artists like Jasper Johns and Roy Lichtenstein preceded the more famous Andy Warhol.

10. Of all these artists, Andy Warhol best understood the media's power to affect people's thinking.

EXERCISE B2-6   Parts of sentences: Review   Before working this exercise, read section B2 in *A Writer's Reference,* Fifth Edition.

_____

Label the function of each italicized word or word group in the following paragraph. Use these codes: subject (S), verb (V), subject complement (SC), direct object (DO), indirect object (IO), and object complement (OC). The first sentence has been done for you.

        S   V   DO

Renoir definitely *had* firm *ideas* about work and about getting along with people. As for work, he believed that *people* everywhere *should use* their *hands* every day. He certainly did, and because he did, *friends* often *called* this hardworking *man* a *workman-painter.* Being called a workman-painter pleased Renoir. Work seemed to be more important to him than the finished product. "The only *reward* for work *is* the *work* itself," he said. He got along with people very well; even his enemies seemed to like him. When his opponents attacked his views, *he* frequently *responded* by suggesting a compromise. *He* freely *offered* other *people* his own successful *techniques* for getting along with his opponents. According to Renoir, *you* certainly *should give* your *enemies* a *chance.* You should also avoid a fight whenever possible. Why? If you avoid fights, your *enemies* often *will become* your *friends.* The *joy* in Renoir's paintings *might be explained* by these approaches to life.

EXERCISE B3-1   Subordinate word groups: Preview   Before working this exercise, read section B3 in *A Writer's Reference,* Fifth Edition.

In the following paragraphs, underline prepositional and verbal phrases once; underline subordinate clauses twice. The first sentence has been done for you; you should find fifteen phrases and five subordinate clauses. Answers to this exercise appear in the back of this book.

Louise Nevelson, who was once called "the finest living American artist," did not earn that title easily.

From her earliest years, she was artistically inclined. Drawing colorful pictures was a favorite childhood pastime. To decorate her room, she collected boxes of pretty rocks, shells, and fabric pieces. Encouraging her artistic interest, her family provided the independence that she needed.

Her husband, Charles Nevelson, who was a wealthy New York businessman, provided her with financial independence, but Louise Nevelson needed personal independence too. The marriage lasted for only eleven years. Then she and her son, Mike, went to her family home. Mike stayed there while his mother studied abroad. Studying, working, and making new friends, Louise developed the self-confidence to follow her own vision.

At times she must have wondered whether or not she had done the right thing. During Louise Nevelson's busiest and most exciting years, her paintings and sculptures were not popular with either the critics or the public. Later, however, her work won critical acclaim, and she was recognized throughout the art world. Rewarded and acclaimed, Louise Nevelson knew that she had made the right decision.

EXERCISE B3-2   **Prepositional phrases**   Before working this exercise, read section B3-a in *A Writer's Reference,* Fifth Edition.

Underline the twenty prepositional phrases in the following sentences. Example:

Children learn many things <u>from their parents</u>.

1. From her builder-father, Louise Nevelson learned an important tradition that had been handed down for generations.

2. Like many other Jewish traditions, it is recorded in the Talmud.

3. The Talmud is a book about Jewish history and laws; it is studied by Jewish scholars.

4. According to the Talmud, Jews should always leave some part of a new house unfinished or unpainted.

5. The unfinished part is there for a reason: It makes people remember the destruction of Jerusalem's second temple.

6. As an adult, Louise moved into a dozen or more "new homes."

7. She sometimes abided by the tradition, but sometimes she forgot about it.

8. Finally, she began at last to understand this tradition that had been handed down for all those years.

9. She saw that over the years she had often left some work unfinished in her studio.

10. Both her work and her life were like her house: Only with an unfinished corner could they grow and change.

EXERCISE B3-3   Verbal phrases   Before working this exercise, read section B3-b in *A Writer's Reference*, Fifth Edition.

The verbal phrase in each sentence has been italicized. Identify each italicized word group as a gerund, a participial, or an infinitive phrase. Example:

> gerund
> ***Working with other artists* made Louise Nevelson very happy.**

1. *Enjoying each other's company,* the members of Ben Shahn's artist group often ate dinner together.

2. Frequently, they would paint a picture right then and there *to celebrate their joy.*

3. *Needing the white tablecloth for their canvas,* the artists would push aside the dishes and food.

4. *Totally involved in their project,* they would look for "paint."

5. *Finding something to use for paint* was not usually a problem.

6. *Making paint from wine drops or pepper or anything else handy* gave them pleasure.

7. Each artist had a chance *to add to the picture.*

8. They enjoyed *adding details to each other's parts of the picture.*

9. *Relaxed and refreshed,* they would leave the restaurant content.

10. No one knows why the restaurant owner allowed them *to do this repeatedly to his tablecloths!*

EXERCISE B3-4   **Prepositional and verbal phrases**   Before working this exercise, read sections B3-a and B3-b in *A Writer's Reference,* Fifth Edition.

Some of the phrases in the following paragraphs are italicized. Label these phrases prepositional (Prep), gerund (Ger), infinitive (Inf), or participial (Part). The first one has been done for you.

Inf

Louise Nevelson's first one-woman show came about because she was determined *to have her work recognized.* Her first choice of a showplace was the Nierendorf Gallery. *Exhibiting there* would put her in the same place where Picasso, Matisse, and Paul Klee had been exhibited. *Showing New York City's best modern art* had helped build a strong reputation for this gallery.

Nevelson went alone to the gallery. First she found Mr. Nierendorf, the gallery's manager. Then, *introducing herself quickly,* she stated quite simply that she wanted an exhibition in his gallery. He was surprised at her forthrightness, but he was also impressed. When he protested that he did not know her work, Nevelson simply invited him *to come and see it.*

He did — the next day — and he offered her a show in twenty-one days. *During the next weeks,* Nevelson got her pieces ready. When the show opened, it was Nierendorf's first exhibition *of an American artist.*

With a few exceptions, art critics liked the show. *Excited by her work,* one critic said that he would have "hailed these sculptural expressions as by surely a great figure among moderns" — if he had not found out the artist was a woman. That left-handed compliment did more harm to the critic than to the artist. Other critics compared her work favorably to Mayan work, *seeing similar forms and rhythms.* Still others commented on the work's "wit" and "zest" and "interest in movement."

Accepted very well, the exhibition was extended past its closing time and gave Nevelson opportunities *to meet some important people* — but not a single piece of art was sold.

EXERCISE B3-5   Subordinate clauses   Before working this exercise, read section B3-e in *A Writer's Reference,* Fifth Edition.

A. Underline the subordinate clauses in the following sentences. Example:

When Louise was part of a struggling young artists' group in New York, she met Diego Rivera.

1. Diego Rivera, who was a Mexican mural painter, introduced Louise Nevelson to other artists and their friends.

2. One of the people whom she met, Marjorie Eaton, became her roommate.

3. Louise also met Ben Shahn while she was working with Rivera.

4. When Louise began working with Ben, she felt at ease with her art for the first time.

5. She knew that she had found her niche.

B. Identify each of the following word groups as a prepositional phrase or a subordinate clause. Example:

    a. After work   *prepositional phrase* _____

    b. After she had worked   *subordinate clause* _____

 6a. Before she went to class   _____

   b. Before her painting class   _____

 7a. Since her happy childhood days   _____

   b. Since she had a happy childhood   _____

 8a. Till the closing bell   _____

   b. Till the bell rang   _____

 9a. After the mural was done   _____

   b. After the sculpture show   _____

10a. Until she mastered the skill   _____

   b. Until her first exhibition   _____

EXERCISE B3-6   Subordinate word groups: Review   Before working this exercise, read section B3 in *A Writer's Reference,* Fifth Edition.

In the following paragraphs, underline prepositional and verbal phrases once; underline subordinate clauses twice. The first sentence has been done for you; you should find twenty more subordinate word groups.

Perhaps <u>becoming a queen</u> is one <u>of every little girl's fantasies</u>. During one experimental stage, Louise Nevelson gave herself that title. She called herself "Queen of the Black Black." While she was experimenting, she used only black materials in her artwork. She decided to make all her surroundings black also. Painting her walls black was the first step. Then she attacked the floors. She did not want to paint them; instead, she used stain to get the desired effect. Stained very dark, the floors did not reflect much light. Her work used no other color, and she insisted that black was "the total color."

At fifty-eight, Louise Nevelson was finally recognized. She became an artist who could expect regular exhibits, sales, and commissions. Museums and collectors bought her work eagerly, paying her well. She was awarded honorary degrees from various universities and accepted invitations to attend White House dinners. She enjoyed receiving these honors, but her greatest pleasure came later.

When Louise Nevelson celebrated her eightieth birthday, her hometown gave her what she had always wanted: The local museum exhibited her work, and the town bestowed a title upon her — "Queen of the City."

EXERCISE B4-1   Sentence types: Preview   Before working this exercise, read section B4 in *A Writer's Reference,* Fifth Edition.

Indicate on the blank after each sentence in the following paragraphs whether the sentence is simple (S), compound (C), complex (CX), or compound-complex (CC). The first blank has been filled for you, and answers to this exercise appear in the back of the book.

Both were famous for breaking with tradition and starting a new way of thinking about art, but Pierre-Auguste Renoir and Louise Nevelson were different in many ways. __C__

A nineteenth-century man born in France, Renoir traveled to Italy to study the Renaissance artists' work; Nevelson, a twentieth-century woman born in America, traveled to Europe to study all kinds of art. _____ Although he devoted several years to drawing, most of Renoir's work was in painting. _____ Nevelson, on the other hand, explored many of the arts besides painting; she worked extensively in music, dance, and sculpture. _____

Renoir loved brightness and bursts of color; she loved darkness and tones of black. _____ He created and finished everything while he was out of doors; she did her work inside a studio. _____ Renoir avoided lines, even blurring outlines to make one part of a painting blend into another. _____ Nevelson was so fond of line that she painted different parts of her sculpture in different colors; she wanted to accentuate the sculpture's form. _____

Unlike Renoir, who liked to paint people and group scenes, Nevelson constructed abstract forms. _____ Using paints and oils, Renoir fashioned homey, identifiable scenes that his viewers could easily recognize. _____ Using discarded milk crates and burned pieces of wood, Nevelson constructed puzzling, enigmatic sculptures different from those of any other artist. _____

EXERCISE B4-2   Sentence types   Before working this exercise, read section B4 in *A Writer's Reference,* Fifth Edition.

A. In the following sentences, underline subordinate clauses. Then determine the sentence type, and indicate it in the blank: simple, compound, complex, or compound-complex. Example:

> **<u>Because Louise Nevelson was always sure of herself,</u> she could not change direction.**
>
> _____ *complex* _____

1. The techniques that the artists Pierre-Auguste Renoir and Louise Nevelson used to handle their anger were quite different. _____

2. Renoir tried to turn anger aside; because he often deflected it with a compromise, the other person seemed to win the argument. _____

3. Once, angry and disappointed at the lack of sales after a major exhibition, Nevelson burned two hundred canvases and all of the sculptures in the show. _____

4. Nevelson said that she used her anger to provide energy on many occasions.

   _____

5. Of course the two never met, but wouldn't it have been fun to watch them together?

   _____

B. Write five sentences of your own of the kind indicated. Underline your subordinate clauses.

6. Simple: _____

7. Compound: _____

   _____

8. Complex: _____

   _____

9. Complex: _____

   _____

10. Compound-complex: _____

    _____

EXERCISE B4-3   Sentence types: Review   Before working this exercise, read section B4 in *A Writer's Reference,* Fifth Edition.

Indicate on the blank after each sentence in the following paragraphs whether the sentence is simple (S), compound (C), complex (CX), or compound-complex (CC). The first blank has been filled for you.

Was there anything that artists Pierre-Auguste Renoir and Louise Nevelson had in common? _CX_ Yes, both showed an interest in art when they were children, and both traveled to another country to study art after they were grown. ____ In addition, although the colors were different, both had periods when they used only one color in their work. ____ And both had to overcome significant odds. ____ Nevelson's problems were mostly emotional and financial, but Renoir's were physical. ____ Renoir's painful arthritis crippled his hands as he grew older; he could paint only by having his brushes tied to his hands. ____

These artists were alike in ways significant to the art world. ____ Both broke free of long-standing accepted traditions in their field and introduced new techniques. ____ Both connected with their viewers in ways that forced the viewers to respond. ____ Both started new ways of looking at things; whether they painted a flowering tree or a stack of burned wood, these artists made viewers see objects differently. ____ They had to fight for and wait for recognition, but both won fame: Renoir and Nevelson were recognized during their lifetimes as artists of particular importance. ____

Answers to Guided Practice and Preview Exercises

EXERCISE S1-1, page 1

Suggested revisions:

In his own time, one famous sixteenth-century man was known only by his given name, "Leonardo." Today he is still known by that single name. But then and now, that name suggests many different roles for its owner: theatrical producer, biologist, botanist, inventor, engineer, strategist, researcher, and artist.

Sixteenth-century Venetian soldiers knew Leonardo as a military strategist. When the Turkish fleet was invading their country, Leonardo suggested conducting surprise underwater attacks and flooding the land that the Turkish army had to cross. Engineers knew him as the man who laid out new canals for the city of Milan. Scientists admired him not only for his precise anatomical drawings but also for his discovery that hardening of the arteries could cause death. To Milan's royal court, Leonardo was the artist who was painting impressive portraits, sculpting a bronze horse memorial to the house of Sforza, and at the same time working on a mural of the Last Supper.

Leonardo saw a three-dimensional *s*-curve in all of nature — the flow of water, the movements of animals, and the flight of birds. We recognize the same *s*-curve today in the spiraling form of DNA. Leonardo invented the wave theory: He saw that grain bending as the wind blew over it and water rippling from a stone cast into it were the same scientific event. It was as easy for him to see this wave in sound and light as to observe it in fields and streams. The math of his day could not explain all his theories, but twentieth-century scientists showed the world that Leonardo knew what he was talking about.

Leonardo saw very clearly that the powers of nature could be destructive and that human beings could be savage. At the same time, he saw a unity holding all life's varied parts together, a unity he could express in his art.

"Leonardo" — it's quite a name!

EXERCISE S2-1, page 5

Suggested revisions:

Mary Wollstonecraft, an eighteenth-century writer, may have been England's first feminist. Her entire life reflected her belief in equal rights for women in all areas of their lives: personal, intellectual, and professional.

From childhood, she never had accepted and never would accept the idea that men were superior to women. As a young girl, she knew that her drinking and gambling father deserved less respect than her long-suffering mother. As an adult, she demanded that society give her the same freedom it gave to men.

Wollstonecraft also demanded that men pay attention to her ideas. She did not argue about an idea. Instead, she gave an example of what she objected to and invited her readers to think about it from various points of view. Working this way, she made few enemies among intellectuals. Indeed, she was attracted to and respected by some of the leading intellectuals of her day. Among them she was as well known on one side of the Atlantic as on the other. Tom Paine, the American orator and writer, probably knew her better than Samuel Johnson, the English writer, did.

Professionally, she was a governess, teacher, and writer. When her father's drinking destroyed the family, she and her sisters started a girls' school. Eventually, financial problems forced the school to close, but not before Mary had acquired enough firsthand experience to write *Thoughts on the Education of Daughters* (1786). As competent as or more competent than other writers of the day, she was a more persuasive advocate for women than most of them.

Modern feminists may find it ironic that current encyclopedia entries for "Wollstonecraft" refer researchers to "Godwin," her married name — where they will find an entry for her longer than the one for her famous husband, William Godwin.

EXERCISE S3-1, page 9

Suggested revisions:

Hearing the name Karl Marx, people usually think of Russia. Marx never lived in Russia at all. Actually, he spent almost all of his adult life in England. He was a political exile for the last half of his life.

Marx lived first in Germany. Born of Jewish parents, he completed his university studies with a Ph.D. at the University of Jena. His favorite professor tried to get Marx an appointment to teach at the university. When that professor was fired, Marx gave up hope of teaching at Jena or any other German university. Because he was denied a university position, Marx had to earn his living as a journalist. He worked briefly as a newspaper editor in Germany.

Next came France, Belgium, and a return to Germany. First Marx and his new bride moved to Paris, where Marx worked for a radical journal and became friendly with Friedrich Engels. When the journal ceased publication, Marx moved to Brussels, Belgium, and then back to Cologne, Germany. He did not hold a regular job, so he tried desperately to earn at least enough money to feed his family.

After living in Paris and Brussels, Marx decided he would settle in London. He and his family lived in abject poverty while Marx earned what little income he could by writing for an American newspaper, the *New York Tribune*.

EXERCISE S4-1, page 13

Suggested revisions:

Do you know how slavery began in America or how it ended? When the *Mayflower* landed in September 1620, slaves were already in America. A Dutch ship had unloaded and sold twenty Africans in Jamestown, Virginia, the year before.

But slavery in America began long before that. Many of the early explorers brought slaves with them to the new land, and some historians claim that one of the men in Christopher Columbus's crew was a slave. From the 1500s to the 1800s, slave ships brought ten million African slaves across the ocean.

Most of the slaves stayed in Latin America and the West Indies, but the southern part of the United States received about six percent of them. Few northerners owned slaves, and opposition to slavery was evident by the time of the American Revolution. Rhode Island prohibited the importation of slaves even before the Revolutionary War. After the war, six northern states abolished slavery at once. Others passed laws to phase out slavery, and even Virginia enacted legislation encouraging slave owners to emancipate their slaves.

But it took a war, a tricky political situation, and a clever former slave to free all slaves. History gives Lincoln the credit for liberating the slaves during the Civil War, and he deserves some credit, but emancipation was not his idea. Originally, no government officials seriously considered emancipation because they were so focused on winning the war to save the Union. But then a very important black man talked to Lincoln and gave him the idea and the reason. This man said that freeing slaves would be good for the war effort and asked if Lincoln would agree to do it. Who was this man? He was Frederick Douglass, fugitive slave and newspaper editor.

EXERCISE S5-1, page 17

Suggested revisions:

Sometimes it's hard to separate fact from fiction, history from folklore. Casey Jones, John Henry, Johnny Appleseed, Uncle Sam, Santa Claus — which of these were real men? We've been told stories about them all of our lives, but are those stories true?

There really was a railroad engineer people called "Casey" Jones; he got that nickname because of his birthplace, Cayce, Kentucky. There really was a "Cannonball" too; it was the Illinois-Central's fast mail train. And there really was a train wreck: Engine Number 382 rammed into some freight cars. The accident was not Casey's fault, and Casey died trying to save his passengers. When workers found his body in the wreckage, his hand was still on the air brake lever. (Air brakes had recently been installed on trains to increase their braking power.)

John Henry was an African American railroad worker of great strength. In legend and song, he died after a timed contest against a steam drill. By using a hammer in each hand, he won the contest. John Henry drilled two holes seven feet deep; the steam drill bored only one nine-foot hole. The real John Henry died on the job too, crushed by rocks that fell from the ceiling of a railroad tunnel.

John Chapman, better known as Johnny Appleseed, was a wealthy and well-liked nurseryman who kept moving his place of business west as the frontier moved west. His boyhood friend Sam Wilson supplied meat to the United States troops during the War of 1812. A worker told a government inspector that the "U.S." stamped on the meat stood for "Uncle Sam." Although it was a joke, it caught on, and Congress made the "Uncle Sam" identification official in the 1960s.

That leaves Santa Claus. As far as historians know now, Santa was not real. But legends say that there was once a man who . . .

EXERCISE S6-1, page 21

Suggested revisions:

No one who knew Albert Einstein as a young child would ever have believed that he might one day be called the smartest man in the world. None of his teachers could have predicted success for him. A shy, slow learner, Albert always got in trouble in class. He consistently failed the subjects he did not like. His family could not have predicted his success either. Albert could not even get to meals on time. Night after night his parents had to postpone dinner until servants, after searching the house and grounds, found the boy. He would be full of apologies but have no explanation to offer for his lateness except that he was "thinking." Once his angry father dangled his big gold watch at Albert and told him to figure out how late he was. Albert, who could not tell time, was fascinated by the tiny magnetic compass hanging from the watch chain. The boy asked so many questions about the compass that he did not eat much dinner anyway. When Albert begged his father to lend him the compass to sleep with, his father let him borrow it. Years later Einstein wondered whether that little compass had been the beginning of his interest in science.

EXERCISE S7-1, page 25

Suggested revisions:

Everyone has heard of Martin Luther King Jr. After studying for the ministry at Boston University and earning a doctorate in theology, he went home to the South to work as a minister. He started working in civil rights and became the most influential leader of that cause in America. When he died, the victim of an assassin's bullet, his name was almost synonymous with "civil rights." Historians and biographers have recorded his leadership in the fight to gain basic civil rights for all Americans. Many people who know of his civil rights work, however, are not aware of his skill as a writer. In addition to his carefully crafted and emotional speeches, King produced other important writing.

Among King's most famous writings is his "Letter from Birmingham Jail." Written to answer a statement published by eight Alabama clergymen that King's work was "unwise and untimely," the letter shows King to be a man who had great patience with his critics. Eager to get these clergymen to accept his point of view, King reminds them that they are clergy. Their goodwill, he says, should help them see that his views hold value. Instead of attacking them personally, he analyzes their arguments and then presents his own views. Does he use many of the emotional appeals for which he is justly famous? No, in this letter King depends on logic and reasoning as the tools to win his argument.

EXERCISE W2-1, page 29

Suggested revisions:

Adam Smith, the founder of modern economics, proposed a theory in the eighteenth century that has made him controversial ever since. This economist, born in Scotland and educated in England, wrote the first complete study of political economy. *The Wealth of Nations* was published in the same year that Americans declared their independence from England — 1776. Smith's book pointed out the interdependence of freedom and order, economic processes, and free-trade laws. Although Smith's thinking did not really affect economic policies significantly during his lifetime, its influence in the next century was considerable. Among economists, "the invisible hand" and "laissez-faire" are synonymous with Smith's name. History has only made Smith's ideas more controversial. Say "Adam Smith" to conservative businesspeople, and they will smile and respond with words like "He was a good man — really understood how business works!" Say "Adam Smith" to liberal reformers, and they will grimace and mutter something like "He was an evil man — really sold the average citizen down the river." Both of these reactions are extreme, but such responses indicate that the controversy aroused by Smith's ideas is still alive.

EXERCISE W3-1, page 33

Suggested revisions:

Three books have shaped economic thinking in the Western world more than any others: Adam Smith's *The Wealth of Nations,* Karl Marx's *Das Kapital,* and John Maynard Keynes's *General Theory.* All three books revolutionized economic thinking, but Keynes's book has influenced America more than the other two.

When President Roosevelt asked him to help the United States deal with its Depression, Keynes investigated causes and cures of unemployment. His theory challenged the "laws" that had supported most economic thinking up to that time.

Economists of the time accepted Adam Smith's "law of the markets." This law stated that supply produces demand — that is, if merchants offer goods, people will buy them. Keynes disagreed, arguing that demand, not supply, keeps an economic system healthy and that unemployment leads to a decline in demand.

Classical economists taught that depressions resulted from lack of goods; Keynes said they resulted from lack of buyers. Classicists said, "If you make it, they will buy." Keynes said, "If they have the money and want the product, they will buy."

Adam Smith's followers believed that the market would correct itself, that if things went too far in one direction, market forces would push them in the other direction. They believed that unemployment would diminish if workers accepted lower wages. They also believed that if businesses lowered prices, people would start buying again and the Depression would end.

Keynes said, "No!" He argued that when businesses lowered prices, they would also cut back on production and lay off workers. The laid-off workers would have no money with which to buy anyone's products, and things would go from bad to worse.

EXERCISE W4-1, page 37

Suggested revisions:

A. In the 1800s, an Englishman named Thomas Robert Malthus became involved in economics. He was very interested in predicting how many more people would be in the world eventually and how much food would be available for them. What he figured out was frightening. He said people kept having children faster than society could produce enough to feed them. There was no way to avoid it. Hard times and wars would kill most people. According to Malthus, famine, plagues, and even wars were necessary to eliminate some excess people so the remainder could have enough food.

B. Robert Malthus proved that population grows faster than food supplies. His thinking led him to oppose any help for poor people. He believed that by relieving the immediate problems of the poor, the government actually made it harder for people to feed their families. Malthus said that if the government subsidized their basic needs, people would only have more children, thus increasing the population even more. Then the inevitable famine or drought would have to eliminate even more people to help a few survive. Everyone from worker to supervisor was caught in the same predicament. It is no wonder that when the English historian Thomas Carlyle finished reading Malthus's theories, he pronounced economics "the dismal science."

EXERCISE W5-1, page 41

Suggested revisions:

Economics is not totally dominated by men. Even in the 1800s, when Thomas Malthus and David Ricardo were the experts, one leading writer about economics was a woman, Jane Marcet. Marcet wrote for the popular press. One of her favorite topics to write about was political economy. In her book *Conversations in Political Economy,* Marcet summarized economic doctrines before 1800. Her aim was different from that of either Malthus or Ricardo. Rather than propounding a new theory of her own, she popularized theories of other people. Twentieth-century women have done more than write about theories that men have proposed. Some of them have taken the initiative to develop their own ideas. Sally Herbert Frankel, for example, made the first official calculations of the Union of South Africa's national income. She is only one of the increasing number of women who make careers in economics.

EXERCISE G1-1, page 47

convey, are, are, are, has, is, seem, enjoy, is, is

EXERCISE G2-1, page 51

Almost everyone has heard about Aesop's fables, but most people know very little about Aesop himself. Most of what we know about Aesop is a mixture of hearsay and conjecture. We do know that he was a slave in Greece. One theory is that before he came to Greece he had lived in Ethiopia for most of his life and that "Aesop" is a much-shortened form of "the Ethiopian."

Aesop was not a storyteller then, though he would have loved to speak well enough to tell a good story. He stuttered so badly that he did not even try to talk. In one story we learn, however, that he could communicate. One day a neighbor brought a gift of figs to Aesop's master. Greatly pleased, the master planned to enjoy them after his bath and directed that they be put in a cool place until he was ready. While the master was lying down in the bath, the overseer and his friends ate the figs. When the master discovered the loss of the figs, the other slaves placed the blame on Aesop. They knew that if Aesop were able to speak, he could defend himself, but they did not fear this stammering slave.

The master ordered that Aesop be flogged. Aesop got the master to delay the punishment briefly. Aesop drank a glass of warm water, ran his fingers down his throat, and vomited only water. Pointing at the overseer, he made gestures that the overseer and his friends should do as he had done. They drank the water, ran their fingers down their throats, and vomited figs.

Although Aesop's cleverness saved him from a flogging, it also made an enemy of the overseer. Aesop discovered a basic truth about life: Being right doesn't always help one to make friends.

EXERCISE G3-1, page 55

Everyone has heard of Dorothy and Toto and their tornado "flight" from Kansas to Oz. Everyone also knows that the Oz adventure was pure fantasy and that it ended happily. But another girl from Kansas took real flights all around the real world. Whenever she landed safely after setting one of her many records, everyone rejoiced and sent congratulations to her. When she disappeared on her last flight, the whole world mourned. Not all pilots can claim they have that kind of following.

Neighbors knew that Amelia Earhart would not be a typical "lady." As a child, Amelia was curious, daring, and self-confident; these traits made her stand out among her peers. When she and her sister Muriel were young, girls were supposed to play with dolls. If girls played baseball or collected worms, they were called "tomboys" and were often punished. Boys and girls even had different kinds of sleds — the girls' sleds were lightweight, impossible-to-steer box sleds.

But the Earhart family lived by its own rules. Amelia's father, whom she depended on for approval, bought her the boys' sled she longed for. Then came many fast trips down steep hills; these trips gave Amelia a foretaste of flying with the wind in her face.

The closest Amelia came to flying was on a home-made roller coaster. She and her friends built it, using an old woodshed for the base of the ride. They started eight feet off the ground and tried to sled down the slope without falling off. No one was successful on the first attempt, but Amelia kept trying until she had a successful ride. Satisfied at last, she declared that the ride had felt "just like flying."

EXERCISE G4-1, page 59

Novelists have often used their storytelling talents to influence people's thinking. Charles Dickens did it in nineteenth-century England. From *David Copperfield* to *Oliver Twist,* book after book depicted the plight of the poor and other really unfortunate members of society. Harriet Beecher Stowe did it in nineteenth-century America, but with hardly as many books. Her *Uncle Tom's Cabin* depicted slavery so well that the book was very influential in causing the Civil War.

Harriet Beecher Stowe considered slavery sinful and wanted her book to help end slavery quickly and peacefully. People first read parts of the novel ten years before the beginning of the war. An abolitionist magazine published it a few chapters at a time, hoping the effect of the story would make readers feel so bad about slavery that they would rally to the abolitionist cause. Many people, reading *Uncle Tom's Cabin* installment by installment, did become convinced that nothing could be worse than living in slavery on a southern plantation.

None of the abolitionists, who devoted their energy to abolishing slavery, expected a perfect world when the book itself was published in 1852. But they certainly hoped that the book would be influential. It was. Of all the novels published that year, it was the best seller on both sides of the Atlantic. Its popularity was good news for the abolitionists. Harriet Beecher Stowe's wish came true.

EXERCISE G5-1, page 63

Suggested revisions:

Four young Englishmen added a word to the world's vocabulary in the 1960s, a word that became synonymous with the 1960s, especially with the music of that time. That word was, of course, "Beatles." The Beatles became the most famous popular musical group of the twentieth century and held the loyalty of many fans into the next century.

The Beatles were popular in Liverpool, England, and in Hamburg, Germany, before they came to America on tour and became world-famous. Liverpool and Hamburg loved the four young men and their music. The Beatles' favorite club was the Cavern in Liverpool, where they hung out together, played day and night, and attracted many fans. A Liverpool disk jockey first called attention to them, and a Liverpool music critic and record store owner became their first manager. The disk jockey called them "fantastic," saying that they had "resurrected original rock 'n' roll." The music critic who became their manager, Brian Epstein, made them shape up as a group. Promoting them, arranging club dates for them, and badgering record companies for them, he was determined to win a recording contract for this exciting new group.

In England, the record buying led to the publicity. In America, the publicity led to the record buying. Everyone wanted copies of the original singles: "Love Me Do," "Please, Please Me," and "From Me to You." In America, audiences made so much noise that no one could hear the music. Crowds of screaming teenagers surrounded the Beatles wherever they went, determined to touch one or more of these famous music makers. Reporters observing the conduct of fans at Beatles' concerts found that they had to invent another word to describe the wild, almost insane behavior of the fans. They called it "Beatlemania."

EXERCISE G6-1, page 69

Suggested revisions:

Have you ever heard of the Wobblies? Not many people have these days. That's a shame, because they did at least two things for which they should be remembered. They probably saved the labor movement in America, and they definitely gave American folk music some of its most unforgettable songs. No one really knows how they got their nickname, but almost everyone knows a song or two that they inspired.

The Wobblies were the members of the Industrial Workers of the World (IWW), a small but militant coalition of radical labor groups. The Wobblies could not get along with the major union groups of the day; in fact, they alienated most of those groups.

Although the major unions disliked the Wobblies immensely, they learned some valuable lessons from them. The first lesson was to avoid getting involved in politics. If there was one thing the Wobblies hated more than capitalism, it was politics. The Wobblies avoided politics for one good reason: They believed that political affiliation caused the death of unions. What else did the major unions learn? They learned to deal realistically with workers' problems. Major unions also learned new recruiting techniques from the Wobblies. In addition, they copied the Wobblies in devoting their energy to nuts-and-bolts issues affecting the workers.

The major unions never recognized their debt to the Wobblies, but the debt was still there for later historians to see. When historians began to compile the story of American labor unions, they finally recognized the contributions of the Wobblies.

EXERCISE T1-1, page 77

Suggested revisions:

The United States has always attracted immigrants. Modern scientists think that the first immigrants arrived at least 25,000 years ago, probably traveling over a land bridge just below the Arctic Circle — from Siberia to Alaska. (The land bridge is no longer there. Scientists think that such a bridge formed during the Ice Age, when much of the water in the ocean froze into tall glaciers. As it froze, it exposed large strips of land. Hunters probably followed animals across this land bridge.)

Descendants of the original immigrants were still here in 1607 when settlers from England arrived in Virginia. These early settlers were followed by many more. In the hundred and forty years that followed, thousands made the trip to America. Crowded onto small wooden boats, they left behind their kinfolk and their history and crossed the Atlantic Ocean. Making such a trip took bravery and faith in the future.

Some of the settlers came for religious reasons; others came to escape poverty or imprisonment. But all of them came hoping for happiness. They were followed by many others with the same goal. Ever since those first immigrants 25,000 years ago, waves of immigrants have continued to arrive on America's shores.

EXERCISE T2-1, page 81

Suggested revisions:

Immigrants have come to the United States from all over the world. Initially, new settlers were mostly European, Irish, or English. By the twentieth century, many Asians had taken the frightening boat trip across the Pacific. Usually the men came first. After they had made enough money for passage, their wives and children were brought over. All were in search of the same good life that earlier European immigrants had sought. Unable to live comfortably in their homelands, a large number of Chinese and Japanese gave them up and settled to the western part of the United States.

These new immigrants worked on the railroads and in the mines. American businesses recruited Chinese labor because it was difficult to find American workers who would accept the wages that were paid. Why did workers decide to come to America anyway? Somehow the idea got started that America was a "golden mountain," where people could pick up gold nuggets after an easy climb. Once they got here, most immigrants worked hard because they hoped to make enough money to bring relatives over to America too.

Before and during World War II, many Germans who had been persecuted by Hitler escaped to America. After the war, thousands of "displaced persons" were welcomed by the United States. Later, refugees from Asia, Africa, Latin America, and the Caribbean wanted to be accepted. Franklin D. Roosevelt once said, "All of our people all over the country, except the pure-blooded Indians, are immigrants or the descendants of immigrants." If Roosevelt were alive today, he would know that his statement is still true.

EXERCISE T3/T4-1, page 89

Suggested revisions:

A descendant of early immigrants to North America played a pivotal role in helping later Americans explore their country. There were tribes of American Indians living all over what is now the United States. Each tribe had its own language and customs. Some tribes raided others and took prisoners who then became the raiding tribes' slaves. That is what happened to a young Shoshone girl now known as Sacagawea.

This girl, like many young Shoshones, had a nickname, "He-toe." "He-toe" was the sound a local bird made, and the girl's movements were so swift that friends thought she resembled that bird. When a raiding party of Hidatsas easily captured this young girl, they named her Sacagawea — "bird woman." The frightened young girl did not try to escape but accepted her role and worked for her captors. After [*or* In] a few months, she had acquired a reputation for good sense and good work.

The tribe married Sacagawea to a white man, Toussaint Charbonneau; she was his second wife. Soon pregnant, this typical Indian wife did the chores and left all decisions to her husband; but inwardly, she longed to explore new places and meet new people. She may have been controlled by her husband, but she never missed a chance to learn whatever she could.

When white men appeared, all the Indians were curious. Sacagawea had never seen a man with yellow hair — or red hair. Nor had she ever seen a black man. All these men were trying to get to the "Big Water" far to the west. They would have to cross mountains that they had not even seen yet. They needed horses, guides, and an interpreter who could speak the Shoshone language. Imagine their surprise when this interpreter, whom they had hoped to find, turned out to be a woman — a young, attractive, Shoshone woman.

EXERCISE P1/P2-1, page 97

If a boy wanted to join the football team at Carlisle Indian School, he had to go through a difficult test. Any boy who wanted to be on the team had to stand at one of the goal lines; all the first-string players stood around the field. When the ball was punted to the new boy, he had to catch it and try to get all the way to the other end zone with it. The team members tried to stop him before he could get very far. Only a few players had ever gotten as far as the fifty-yard line, so "Pop" Warner, coach at the Carlisle Indian School, considered it a good test.

One day a quiet Indian boy surprised Pop. The boy caught the ball, started running, wheeled away from the first players who tried to stop him, shook off the others, and ran the ball all the way to the opposite goal line. Convinced that the player's success was an accident, the coach ordered him to run the play again. Brusquely, the coach spoke to the players and reminded them that this workout was supposed to be tackling practice. Jim, the nineteen-year-old six-footer, simply said, "Nobody tackles Jim." Then he ran the ball to the goal line a second time.

Well, almost no one tackled Jim Thorpe successfully for many years. Life itself got him down and made him fumble more often than his football opponents did, but he was usually able to recover and go on. The first blow was the death of his twin brother while the two boys were still in grade school. This tragedy was followed by others; by the time Jim was twenty-five, he had lost his brother, his mother, and his father to death. They left him a Native American heritage: His father was half Irish and half Native American, and his mother was the granddaughter of a famous Indian warrior named Chief Black Hawk.

Fortunately or unfortunately, along with his Native American heritage came great pride and stoicism. That pride kept him silent when the greatest blow of all came: He was forced to return the Olympic medals he had won in 1912 because he was declared to be not an amateur. He dealt stoically with his personal tragedies. When infantile paralysis struck his son, Jim Thorpe disappeared for a few days to deal with the tragedy alone. His stoicism also saw him through a demotion to the minor leagues and sad years of unemployment and poverty before his death.

Even death's tackle may not have been totally successful: After Jim Thorpe's death, his Olympic medals were returned, and a town was named after him.

EXERCISE P3-1, page 105

When Cheryl Toussaint came in second in a race she had never planned to run, she started on a road that led to the Olympics and a world record.

Cheryl Toussaint began running almost by accident one day when she went to watch a city-sponsored track meet in Brooklyn, New York. During the preliminaries, the officials announced an "open" race; it was one that anyone could enter. Cheryl wanted to enter, but she was dressed in a skirt and sandals. Four things made her run: One friend traded shoes with her, another let her borrow jeans, several teased her by calling her "chicken" if she didn't run, and one girl dared her to run. Coming in second in that race led this teenager to many places, including Munich, Germany; Toronto, Canada; and Montreal, Canada.

There were, however, many races to run and lessons to learn. Cheryl joined the all-female Atoms Track Club, and she began training under Coach Fred Thompson. Like most coaches, Fred had his own way of testing newcomers. He watched a new runner carefully; however, he gave her no special attention. Instead, he just gave her orders one after another. He would tell Cheryl to run laps, go through exercises, and do practice starts; but he would never comment on how she performed. If the newcomer endured the hard, time-consuming workouts without encouragement or praise, Thompson was sure that she was ready for real coaching.

Cheryl quit after two months; for six more months she stayed out. During that time she thought about her attitude toward work, her poor record at school, her pleasure in running, and her lack of goals. When she returned, Thompson welcomed her back. Coach Thompson knew how special Cheryl was. He not only convinced her she was college material but pushed her to achieve the highest goal of the amateur athlete — the Olympics.

EXERCISE P4-1, page 109

In 1951, Althea Gibson broke the color barrier in women's tennis and became admired all over the world. No one who knew her as a teenager would have predicted her success. By the time Althea Gibson reached her teens, her record showed three indications of trouble: running away from home, dropping out of school, and losing the one job she had been able to find. To survive in her neighborhood, Althea depended on a small welfare allowance, occasional handouts, and plain old luck. She listed her skills as the following: good bowler, great two-on-two basketball player, and fast paddleball player. Even after she began playing tennis and moving in upper-class Harlem society, she resented the efforts of the society ladies to improve her. They busied themselves with tasks such as correcting her manners and restricting her behavior. Looking back, she later summed up her attitude: She [or she] said she wasn't ready to study about "how to be a fine lady." At eighteen, she finally got a waitress job, a congenial roommate, and a good friend.

EXERCISE P5-1, page 113

During the 1990 troubles in Panama, American television and newspaper reporters had an exciting piece of news. They reported that for the first time American female soldiers had been engaged in actual combat. Acting as her soldiers' leader, Captain Linda Bray led her troops into combat. Names of two additional women who were involved in combat, Staff Sergeant April Hanley and PFC Christina Proctor, were reported in the newspapers. Theirs were the only names reported, although other women also took part.

It wasn't the first time an American woman had fought in an American battle, but it's not likely that many people are aware of that fact. The Civil War had its female fighters too. Loreta Janeta Velazquez fought for the Confederates in the Civil War after her husband's death. Like many other women whose husbands were killed in that war, she must have asked herself, "Who's going to take his place in battle?" The decision to fight was hers alone. Someone is sure to ask how that was possible, even in those days. Military I.D.s were not very sophisticated in the 1860s. Someone's willingness to fight was that person's major qualification, and each fighting unit needed to replace its losses as fast as possible. Velazquez simply disguised herself in men's clothing, found a troop needing replacements, and joined the fight. Loreta Janeta Velazquez was Linda Bray's Civil War predecessor.

EXERCISE P6-1, page 117

1. The doctor answered, "You can do nothing but pray."
2. When the bandages were removed and the shades were opened to let in the bright sunlight, the doctor asked, "What do you see?"
3. "Nothing," said the boy. "I see nothing."
4. The village priest said, "I have recently seen a remarkable school." He had just returned from a trip to Paris.
5. "In this school," he added, "blind students are taught to read."
6. "You didn't say 'read,' did you?" asked the boy's father.
7. The boy responded to the priest's words as if they were a trick of some kind: "Now you are joking with me. How can such a thing be possible?"
8. The boy, Louis, thought it would be great fun to visit that school someday.
9. His father promised, "We will go soon, Louis."
10. And so it happened that ten-year-old Louis Braille entered the National Institute for Blind Youths and began the long effort to erase the fear people had of even the word "blind" [or blind].

EXERCISE P7-1, page 122

Suggested revisions:

The most famous woman in America is Miss Liberty — a 450,000-pound, 154-foot resident of New York City. For people all over the world, the Statue of Liberty symbolizes America. Yet the idea for the statue did not come from America, England, or even New York itself. Where did the idea come from? It came from France. Three men can claim the credit for construction of Miss Liberty: Frédéric-Auguste Bartholdi, sculptor; Alexandre-Gustave Eiffel, structural engineer; and Richard Morris Hunt, architect. France gave the statue to the United States, and the United States provided the pedestal on which it stands.

Two Americans contributed significantly to the statue. The first was Russian immigrant Joseph Pulitzer, then owner and publisher of the *New York World*. He led several fundraising efforts and urged every citizen to give what he or she could to help build the pedestal. The second American who contributed significantly was Emma Lazarus. She wrote the famous lines on the bronze plaque inside the statue. Her three-word title "The New Colossus" (huge statue) alludes to a statue built in the harbor of Rhodes in ancient Greece. The most quoted lines from "The New Colossus" are probably these: "Give me your tired, your poor, / Your huddled masses yearning to breathe free."

EXERCISE M1/M2/M3-1, page 127

Everyone has heard of Christopher Columbus, but not many people know much about him. Most people remember that he discovered America in A.D. 1492. Some people know that he had three ships, but they might not be sure whether they could name them. (The ships were the *Niña*, the *Pinta*, and the *Santa María*.) A few people might even remember that Columbus thought he had found the Indies. And those with great self-confidence might be willing to guess at the number of trips he made to his India. (It was four.) Probably no one would be familiar with his favorite word, *adelante*.

If they were asked what Columbus was trying to prove with his expensive journey, most people would reply that he was trying to prove the world was round. They would be wrong. If they were asked what Columbus meant by "the Indies," they would probably say "India." They would be wrong again. If they were asked what Columbus's rank was, they would most likely say "captain." They would be wrong again. If they were asked what his sailors feared most, a number of them would reply,

"They feared that the boats would fall off the edge of the earth." And they would be wrong again.

Isn't it strange that people can be so ignorant about a well-known man like Columbus?

EXERCISE M4/M5/M6-1, page 131

After being feted, feasted, and honored on his return from his first voyage across the ocean, Columbus must have told and retold the story of his trip. He would have told listeners how, after the ships had sailed for three weeks, his men threatened to turn back because they had never sailed so far west before. Columbus, sure of his special calling as an explorer, promised them that they would sight land within three days. On the evening of the third day, at ten o'clock, he thought he saw a light and alerted a nearby servant. Both of them lost sight of it almost at once. But at two o'clock the next morning, a cannon shot sounded from the *Pinta.* "Land! Land!" cried the sailors. Columbus had kept his promise.

Retelling the story of his voyage, Columbus would have described the beautiful island that the ships first landed on. He named it San Salvador. He would have told how, at every island he and his men visited, natives had flocked to the boats to see the strangers; for example, one day, more than a thousand people had come in just one hour. Columbus spent three months exploring and setting up a fort before leaving for the return trip to Spain. And on their return, eight months later, he and his crew received a royal welcome.

Yes, he had had a few problems on the trip out, and the return trip had been very hard, but the memories of that first voyage were indelibly imprinted on Columbus's brain.

EXERCISE B1-1, page 137

readers, N; are, MV; of, P; its, PN; and, C; or, C; formal, ADJ; starts, MV; simply, ADV; with, P; should, HV; everyone, PN; about, P; certain, ADJ; when, C; them, PN; acts, MV; government, N; bold, ADJ; been, HV

EXERCISE B2-1, page 145

group, S; had, V; problem, DO; they, S; went, V; They, S; gave, V; paintings, IO; bursts, DO; lovers, S; were surprised, V; artists, S; made, V; scenes, DO; bright, OC; would pour, V; sunshine, S; Were, V; paintings, S; bright, SC; cheerful, SC; painters, S; are admired, V; forms, S; are, V; examples, SC; Both, S; showed, V; viewers, IO; objects, DO

EXERCISE B3-1, page 151

Verbal phrases: Drawing colorful pictures; To decorate her room; Encouraging her artistic interest; Studying, working, and making new friends; to follow her own vision; Rewarded and acclaimed

Prepositional phrases: From her earliest years; of pretty rocks, shells, and fabric pieces; with financial independence; for only eleven years; to her family home; At times; During Louise Nevelson's busiest and most exciting years; with either the critics or the public; throughout the art world

Subordinate clauses: that she needed; who was a wealthy New York businessman; while his mother studied abroad; whether or not she had done the right thing; that she had made the right decision

EXERCISE B4-1, page 157

Compound; Complex: Although he devoted several years to drawing (subordinate clause); Compound; Compound; Compound-complex: while he was out of doors (subordinate clause); Simple; Compound-complex: that she painted different parts of her sculpture in different colors (subordinate clause); Complex: who liked to paint people and group scenes (subordinate clause); Complex: that his viewers could easily recognize (subordinate clause); Simple